Calm Working
SPACES

Calm Working
SPACES

Lorrie Mack

MARSHALL PUBLISHING ■ LONDON

A Marshall Edition
Conceived, edited and designed by
Marshall Editions Ltd
The Orangery
161 New Bond Street
London W1Y 9PA

First published in the UK in 2000
by Marshall Publishing Ltd

ISBN 184028 350 5

Originated in Singapore by Chroma Graphics
Printed and bound in South Korea by Samhwa Printing Co., Ltd.

Project editor   Jane Chapman
Art editor   Joyce Mason
Picture researcher   Jess Walton
Managing editor   Anne Yelland
Managing art editor   Helen Spencer
Editorial director   Ellen Dupont
Art director   Dave Goodman
Production   Amanda Mackie
Editorial coordinator   Ros Highstead
Editorial assistant   Emily Salter
DTP editor   Lesley Gilbert

Front cover photography: Fritz von der Schulenburg/The Interior
Archive (Designer: John Stefanidis);
Back cover photography: *a*=above; *b*=below; *l*=left; *c*=centre; *r*=right
ar Camera Press; *cr* Andrew Wood/Interior Archive (Designer: Peter
Wylly); *br* Paul Ryan/ International Interiors (Architects: Hairi and Hairi);
bl Fritz von der Schulenburg/Interior Archive

Contents

Introduction

In the space of a single generation, communications technology has revolutionized our lives completely. Often it's difficult to remember a time when it wasn't possible to dispatch the printed word across the world instantly, access information on any subject, order goods and services at the touch of a button, and communicate with people and organizations around the world.

Of all the social changes this revolution has brought about, one of the most significant is the huge increase in the number of people now working at home, either full or part time. And as computer technology grows in capacity and sophistication while shrinking in size and cost, home working will become a viable option for a growing section of the population. Certainly, compared to the traditional pattern of daily commuting, this way of life offers vastly increased freedom, flexibility, comfort and control, and a dramatic reduction in travelling time, career pressure and corporate regimentation. And – an important factor for many people – working from home gives people the opportunity to spend more time with the family.

■ *On this wide, sunny half landing, a well-stocked library corner makes good use of the area under the stairs. Note the shelves, which differ in height and width in order to accommodate the varied collection of books.*

■ *A powerful laptop, a traditional desk lamp and a set of lidded filing boxes made from woven grass have transformed this old farmhouse table into a compact and welcoming home office (below).*

QUALITY OF LIFE

In addition to convenience and autonomy, home working has a great deal to offer in emotional terms, providing insulation from many of the principal irritations of office life – the politics and personality clashes that can so effectively fray nerves and shorten tempers. For some groups of workers – the disabled, carers and single parents, for example – the opportunity to work at home can totally transform their lives. And it's not only workers who benefit. Many employers, too, notice that productivity is often higher, and overheads lower, when their staff – salaried or casual – are not all assembled in uninspiring, expensive commercial spaces.

Working at home also allows you to spend your days in an environment you have created specifically to suit the job you do and the way you want to do it. You are completely free to express your personality by surrounding yourself with colours, styles and design details that you would never encounter in a business context, where often a wide variety of different people and

■ *Providing a dramatic contrast in terms of both size and style, this spacious studio, with its purpose-designed furniture, houses a small home-based business (opposite).*

disciplines have to be catered for. (Of course, those who work in a conventional office, if their employers encourage individual creativity, can make use of the ideas in this book to define and personalize their own space.)

NEW MARKETS

To fill the phenomenal and rising demand, the home-working revolution has given birth to a whole new retail sector: the SOHO market (small office, home office). Where once the only office furniture and equipment you could buy was intended for commercial (contract) use, now there is a wide choice of affordable ranges specially designed and scaled to suit a domestic setting.

The burgeoning popularity of home working has also influenced the housing sector, where more and more new homes are being built with a designated study or office included on the original plan. And one of the most significant areas of growth in the property market involves what are known as live/work units. This term describes conventional houses or flats that are constructed (or converted from industrial or commercial buildings) to include an integral but full-sized and self-contained work space, often with its own entrance to ensure a professional separation between home and business.

■ *The key to this bright, stylish live/work room is flexibility: a movable screen that defines the office area; adjustable clamp lights that provide illumination where it's most needed; and a desk that can be wheeled out of sight when it's time to relax.*

■ *You don't have to be running a full-time business from home to appreciate the benefits of having a quiet place where you can deal with day-to-day correspondence. Even the most tiresome paperwork will be easier to face if you can set aside a peaceful corner such as this writing desk.*

"I NEVER FOUND THE COMPANION THAT WAS SO COMPANIONABLE AS SOLITUDE."
HENRY THOREAU

A PRIVATE PLACE

It's not only home workers who benefit from a well-equipped office area; every household runs more smoothly when its members have access to a purpose-designed place in which to tackle correspondence, administer accounts and pursue special interests and hobbies. And remember that people who perform these tasks by hand-writing letters, filling out cheques and finding information in books and magazines have just as much need for a calm working space as those who send e-mails, transfer funds electronically and spend hours tapping into the Internet.

Whichever category you fall into, this book will help you to achieve your ideal work space – one that meets your needs, reflects your personality and blends gracefully with the rest of your home. Practical advice on everything from floor planning and security precautions to choosing the most ergonomic chair and flexible lighting system will ensure that working from home is a productive and comfortable experience. A section on style will show you how you can introduce elements such as inventive storage, colour and scent to personalize your space and create a stress-free environment. Stunning photographs and a series of case studies will guide you through the design challenges and fire your imagination.

Whether you are starting from scratch or overhauling an existing work area, *Calm Working Spaces* will make it possible for you to create an environment that represents the ideal balance between your business and your personal life: each one complete, independent and successful, but close enough in space and in spirit to overlap and interrelate to the enrichment of both.

■ *In order to cater for a couple who share their domestic paperwork, these simple armchairs face each other across the large table in an arrangement inspired by an old-fashioned partners' desk.*

PART ONE

Taking stock

Any task approached in a calm, organized manner is a task half conquered. Whether you're negotiating a complex business deal, filling in an insurance claim or a tax return, or simply writing thank-you notes, you will perform more efficiently and take infinitely more pleasure in what you do if you have a well-ordered, comfortable and visually appealing place in which to work.

As with any design project, you should begin the process of creating a successful work space by assessing your needs so that you can plan for them. What exactly will you do here? Will you be working at home on a regular basis? How do you work? What equipment and materials will you need? Once established, this information will help you decide where to locate your work space, what should go into it and how you can arrange it for maximum ease and efficiency.

■ *In this unusual mezzanine work space, the overpowering impression is of light: streaming through the vast windows and doors, bouncing off the white walls and pale timber and creating dramatic reflections in the glass desk. At the edge of the floor, a balustrade made from rows of yacht rigging provides a safety barrier.*

"THE IDEAL OF HAPPINESS HAS ALWAYS TAKEN MATERIAL FORM IN THE HOUSE, WHETHER COTTAGE OR CASTLE; IT STANDS FOR PERMANENCE AND SEPARATION FROM THE WORLD."

SIMONE DE BEAUVOIR

Making plans

Before you begin to design your working space, set aside some time to think about the nature of the work that will be done there. Broadly, it should fall into one of two categories: occasional use, which takes in things like writing letters and paying bills, or regular use, which includes any kind of income-producing activity or serious study course.

DOMESTIC DETAILS

Clearly, there is less need for meticulous planning and design when it comes to a work area that will be used occasionally than there would be for a comparable space occupied full time. You'll gain enormously, though, by investing thought and resources in even the most modest home office. Paperwork such as bills, pensions and insurance policies become troublesome and worrying when they're lost or forgotten, and providing an orderly place to store and deal with them is the best way to keep them under control. It's a great pity, too, when corresponding with family and friends is a chore that you avoid for as long as possible. A peaceful corner, a well-appointed desk and a comfortable chair may encourage you to see writing letters and sending cards as a pleasurable activity to look forward to at the end of a stressful day.

■ *For conveying personal messages, no sophisticated technology will ever equal the charm and intimacy of a hand-written note. The owner of this delightful correspondence desk keeps a good stock of stationery supplies.*

BUSINESS STUDIES

If you're planning to run a business from home, begin by asking yourself exactly what your work will consist of and what environment and supplies you will need in order to do it. Will you be putting in a full day at your desk, or is much of your time going to be spent on the road – seeing clients, perhaps, or doing research? Are you expecting regular visitors to your home? Will you need extra help at busy periods? Does your occupation (or your personality) require a noise-free environment, or do you like to hear the buzz of household activities while you work? Will you need privacy for regular meetings or telephone conversations? Try to assess how your business will progress in the next couple of years. Do you foresee an expansion that will require more space and equipment or perhaps extra staff?

Efficiently organized on a small side table, this unobtrusive work space tucks neatly into a quiet corner between the foot of the bed and the high sunny window.

CALM WORKING SPACES

■ *Choosing a range of fitted home-office furniture allows you to squeeze the maximum amount of storage capacity under a continuous expanse of work surface. Also, the resulting visual cohesion helps to create an impression of neatness and organization. Here, accessories like the printer and its paper supply are housed in a purpose-designed drawer.*

■ *In this converted loft (above), the desk assumes an almost altar-like position under the huge, pointed arch that dominates the space. On the left, a bright beach-hut storage unit echoes the same shape while dispelling any hint of architectural solemnity.*

■ *A modestly proportioned bedroom has been turned into a private consulting room, which manages to look calmly professional while at the same time being comfortable and welcoming for clients (opposite).*

Think about your circumstances – now and in the future. If you are intending to move on within a year or two, freestanding furniture is likely to be a wiser choice than extensive built-in fittings. Similarly, those who rent – even under a tenancy agreement that permits such alterations – may not feel inclined to install expensive built-in shelving or work surfaces in property that belongs to someone else. Even if your accommodation – rented or private – is temporary, however, there are some items, such as a well-designed chair and lighting, that will always repay their investment in terms of productivity and comfort.

What about storage provision? Will your job involve significant quantities of paper, files or reference books? Do you need to store anything bulky, like samples of merchandise or materials? Which items are in constant use and should therefore live within easy reach, and which can be housed further away – perhaps even in another room?

Will you need to use a computer, telephone, fax machine, photocopier, printer or lightbox, and if so, how often and for how long? If most of your business is done on the telephone or the Internet, you will have to

CALM WORKING SPACES

■ *Designed to maximize the limited floor area in this spare room/work space, the unusual wedge-shaped desk fits neatly between two storage units. At one end, the work surface is deep enough to accommodate a pedestal storage unit underneath; at the other end, the desk's gentle taper leaves plenty of clearance for the sofa bed to be pulled out.*

arrange a separate, dedicated line, whereas if you use the phone only reasonably frequently, a desk extension to the existing line will probably do. If, however, you make only four or five calls a day, you could free your work surface by putting the phone on another table or shelf. (If you use the phone less than that, and you are within hearing distance of the main household extension, you may not require a separate extension at all.)

Any item you need only occasionally might be more wisely located elsewhere, especially when space is tight; if your correspondence tends to be infrequent and non-urgent, a fax machine can serve you just as efficiently

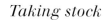

"A HOUSE IS A MACHINE FOR
LIVING IN."
                    LE CORBUSIER

in a less-busy room. To accommodate any kind of equipment in frequent use,
however, you should provide a stable surface positioned at an accessible
height fairly near to your work station, with plenty of power points.

What about display facilities? Would it help to have things like schedules,
price lists, maps or visual references pinned up in front of you instead of
tucked away in a drawer or file?

Whether you work or study full or part time, a computer is likely to play a
dominant role in your activities. If virtually all your work is done at your
machine, you may need little more surface area around it than is taken up by

■ *In another contemporary reworking of the traditional partners' desk, the custom-made fittings in this skilfully planned home office (above) incorporate two L-shaped work stations, a round meeting table, a wall-mounted storage unit and extensive open shelving.*

a keyboard. When this is the case, a full-sized desk might be unnecessary, and most of the valuable space within easy reach can be devoted to other items of equipment or storage. If, on the other hand, written work and piles of paper play an important part in your labours, a work surface that is too small and constantly cluttered will produce not only permanent muddle but a high level of anxiety as well.

And finally, where is your work space in relation to the kitchen? If the distance is so great that getting yourself a cup of tea or coffee is a significant interruption to your work, try to make room for a kettle and some mugs to avoid wasting your time and breaking your concentration.

The right location

In principle, there are several possible sites for a home office, but the most practical tend to involve giving over part of an existing room; designing a room with dual, alternating functions; setting aside a separate room as a full-time office; or adapting a previously underused area like a hallway or landing. Home workers with the inclination and the means to make a more serious commitment might consider converting a garage or an attic, or even constructing a separate out-building from scratch. You may feel that the size or layout of your home limits your choice, but before you settle on the most obvious option, make sure you've investigated all the workable alternatives –

■ *To screen off the business end of a multi-purpose room, hang full-length curtains from a ceiling-fixed track. In this cool, fresh scheme, prettily spotted voile divides the sleeping and working areas without blocking the light completely.*

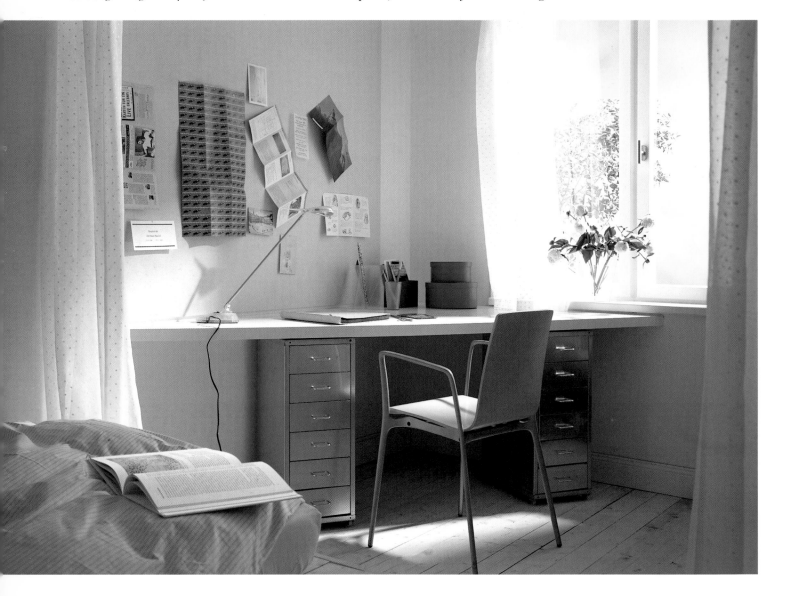

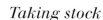

■ *Situated well away from the bustle of family life, a separate home office tucked under the eaves offers maximum peace and privacy plus the chance to leave your work environment behind at the end of the day (left and below).*

there may be more than you imagine. Depending on the nature of your work, you might even decide not to become established in one particular spot. The market is now flooded with portable equipment offering the home worker the flexibility of being able to move around and set up base quickly and efficiently. (In many corporate offices, this way of working, known as 'hot desking', is becoming increasingly popular.)

So, instead of being tied to the same work space day after day, you could perhaps find a secluded corner when concentration is vital and then move to a more central location when you want to keep an eye on the children. With a laptop computer and a mobile phone at your disposal, you might decide to set up base outdoors when the weather is good, and then decamp to a place by the fire when the temperature drops. Another advantage of the floating office is that you can easily take your work on the road when necessary.

A WORKING CORNER

If purloining part of an existing room seems to be the most obvious choice, you will still need to think carefully about which room this will be.

Working in your bedroom often makes the most sense in terms of space, and when your intended use is essentially occasional, this arrangement works very well. Certainly, most bedrooms are empty during the day and many have room to spare. Children and teenagers in particular need a place to study away from the bustle of family life; if space is tight, investigate the possibility of placing the bed on a raised platform to free the area underneath for a desk and chair.

While many people are happy to work for extended periods in the bedroom, for others the thought of spending so much time inside the same four walls is intolerable. Remember, too, that finding the discipline to focus on your work each morning and – equally importantly – to leave it behind again in the evening is difficult for most people who work at home in any location, but the transition is even trickier when your work space and sleeping area are one and the same. You may even find that your sleep pattern is affected, especially if your business is going through a difficult time. Decide whether you would feel comfortable waking up every morning to the sight of your computer.

Another popular site for a home office is the living room – a solution that can work well in single-person households. As well as available space, there is likely to be scope for convenient sharing of facilities such as telephone and bookshelves between your work and your personal life; a dining table can double up as an extra desk or meeting area, for example, and a comfortable sofa and chairs near the nerve centre are ideal for informal discussions with

■ As well as defining different activity areas, raising the floor in one part of a multi-function room offers a range of practical advantages. In this vast studio/living space (below), the change of level improves the view and makes the most of the streaming sunlight. Inside an enclosed bar (below right), a similar alteration has placed the original granite surface at the perfect height to serve as a desk-cum-drafting board for the designer who works here.

clients or colleagues. If you share your home with others, though, this arrangement is less likely to be satisfactory. Even in an adults-only household, the most conscientious of workers would find it hard to resist distractions from surrounding movement and conversation, and co-habitees are unlikely to appreciate being asked to tone down their activities for the benefit of the stressed home worker. When children are part of the equation, the situation is probably impossible, so you must find somewhere else to set up shop.

A spacious kitchen, especially one with a large table, is another popular option. Here again, paying bills, sending e-mails and writing letters amid the bustle of family life is perfectly possible; running a full-time business from the kitchen – no matter what its size – is practical only when the room is empty and quiet for a good part of the day.

Architecturally, the ideal arrangement for accommodating two permanent functions is an L-shape: your office could fit neatly into the short arm of the L and, if necessary, be screened off from the rest of the room with a pair of folding doors or a floor-to-ceiling curtain. One end of a long, narrow room would lend itself to the same treatment. If neither of these options is workable, try fitting your work space into a corner so that, if necessary, you can hide it away behind a folding screen.

CALM WORKING SPACES

"A HOUSE IS NO HOME UNLESS
IT CONTAINS FOOD AND FIRE
FOR THE MIND AS WELL AS
FOR THE BODY."
MARGARET FULLER

■ *The ample proportions of a 19th-century drawing room provide plenty of space for a cosy living area and an efficient home office to exist happily side by side. Two large sofas cater for informal business meetings as well as relaxation.*

■ *A huge, old refectory table acts as both drawing and display surface for the textile designer who lives and works in this airy Milan apartment/showroom.*

DOUBLE DUTY

In terms of peace, privacy and convenience, as well as space, the next step up from working in the corner of a main room is adapting a room that is not in constant use to fulfil two alternating functions. Ideal candidates for this treatment are guest rooms and separate dining rooms. The secret of a successful dual scheme is to make an appropriate match between the two sets of demands. A busy office can happily share accommodation with guest quarters that are rarely occupied, for example: simply treat the room primarily as a work place but include in your furnishings a sofa bed, day bed or divan, a small table for night-time accessories and a few hooks or a coat rack.

At the other end of the scale, trying to do a serious full-time job with a steady stream of house guests popping in and out will produce unacceptable levels of frustration, so if your home sometimes feels like a hotel, locate your work space elsewhere. A compact desk or writing table in the spare room, however, stocked with paper, envelopes and stamps, would be welcomed by most visitors, and when the room is unoccupied, permanent residents can take advantage of this peaceful corner to deal with personal correspondence.

In the same way, a dining room that is used only on special occasions can make a perfect home office. If there isn't enough space here to store your best cutlery, china, glass and table linen as well as office supplies and equipment,

keep the tableware in the kitchen or wherever there's room; the inconvenience of carting these things from room to room is bearable if it isn't necessary too often. Most importantly, install a large table that will serve as both desk and dining surface. When it is time for a birthday dinner or Christmas lunch, you can simply tidy the files away, clear the desk and shift the room into catering mode. Here again, the steps necessary to turn a well-planned work space into a stylish dining room are little trouble to undertake once in a while, but if your dining room is in daily use, resist the temptation to earmark it for anything more ambitious than occasional use as an office. No matter how tempting the space may be, clearing away your work at the end of every day, then setting it out again each morning, will be time consuming for even the most organized and disciplined of home workers.

The double bed in this dual-purpose room has a simple, tailored elegance that does not compromise the overall impression of stylish professionalism.

A ROOM OF YOUR OWN

The perfect environment for any kind of work or study is undoubtedly a separate room – a quiet, private sanctuary where you can immerse yourself completely in your tasks, then close the door on them at the end of the working day. You may be able to commandeer a room for this purpose by doubling up on the functions of the others: move a table and chairs into the living room, for instance, to free the dining room, or persuade two children to share sleeping accommodation so that a bedroom becomes available. Using a more sophisticated version of the same principle, you might even be able to liberate the kitchen by moving its function to one end of a large living room, fitting stylish units and appliances to create a loft-like open-plan space. Alternatively, divide a single spacious room into two smaller ones with a new partition wall.

If you have a choice about which room in your home to occupy, consider all the relevant options. Clearly, an office should have plenty of space and light, but its situation in the building is important for other reasons as well. If you use expensive equipment such as a computer, you may be better off working at the back of the house or on an upper floor, rather than in a ground-level, front-facing room where opportunist thieves may be tempted by the window display.

If your business involves lots of collections and deliveries, or when visitors call frequently, you'll appreciate being near the front door. A noisy fax machine or printer, especially if it's active during the evening, should be located as far as possible from sleeping children, and this also applies to a business phone, if you use it regularly and at length in the evening.

■ *While some creative people are inspired by a cheerful jumble of colours, shapes, surfaces and work in progress (below), others produce their best work in an ordered and uncluttered environment that focuses all their attention on the project in hand (opposite).*

"THE HAPPIEST OF ALL LIVES IS
A BUSY SOLITUDE."

VOLTAIRE

■ *The richly patterned rugs, shiny black
surfaces and distinctively styled desk, chair
and lamp give this converted industrial
space a subtle oriental look. Set into the
smooth plaster, unobtrusive recessed
spotlights bathe the room with warm,
flattering light.*

■ *Lined with colourwashed timber cladding, this understairs cubbyhole acts as a miniature studio for an amateur calligrapher. The desk, shelf units and wall lamp have all been chosen to blend discreetly into the background (below).*

STOLEN SPACES

Some of the most ingenious – and efficient – working spaces are carved out of underused (or completely wasted) architectural nooks and crannies. A spacious entrance hall, for example, may be able to accommodate much more than an umbrella stand and a row of boots, while a wide landing may provide exactly the peaceful, empty corner you're looking for.

In older homes, the area under a main staircase has often been boxed in to make a cupboard (which rapidly fills with junk). If you have a staircase like this and can spare the storage area, see if you can rip out what's there and replace it with a small-scale work area. Alternatively, a roomy built-in cupboard or closet, with the addition of a fitted work surface and some shelves, can make a compact office that disappears as soon as the door is closed.

In some buildings, the greatest expanse of unused space is at ceiling level. When a room (or even a stairwell) is high enough, you can occasionally gain valuable floor space the size of a small room by constructing a raised gallery or mezzanine level. Although this kind of structure doesn't offer the perfect privacy and quiet of a closed-off room, it will provide a permanent place to work and will give you a vital sense of psychological separateness from the rest of your home and the people you share it with.

■ *With a little ingenuity, functional work spaces can be squeezed into the smallest areas. Here the surface has been specially cut to fit an awkward recess in a tiny box room. Two filing cabinets fit neatly under one half of the desk (right).*

■ *On this lofty mezzanine overlooking the front door and garden beyond, a modern classic trestle table by Castiglioni serves as* a desk, while at the side a row of pedestal storage units accommodates stationery and filing.

The steeply sloping walls of this sunny top-floor studio set a strongly geometric style that is echoed throughout the room's design, from the strong diagonal lines of the floorboards to the triangular desk and the angled peninsular unit that screens the tiny kitchen from the rest of the room.

STARTING FROM SCRATCH

When there is nowhere in your home that ingenuity, adaptation and skilled decorating can transform into an adequate work space, it may be time to call in the professionals – an architect and a builder – to create one from scratch. In some cases, it's possible to accomplish this within the original structure by converting an attic, garage or basement, but in all cases you will need to consider making some structural alterations. These could include anything from installing windows and constructing inner surfaces such as floors, walls and ceilings to adding insulation or plumbing or re-routeing electrical wiring.

Attics are a popular choice for an office, since the space at the top of the house is unlikely to be in use for anything but storage. Basements, although usually offering plenty of space, can be more complicated to convert. Being situated even partly below ground level, with little natural ventilation, basements can be prone to damp and mustiness. As natural light is usually limited or non-existent, you will also need to install a good lighting system.

If your home presents no possible area for exploitation, consider building an extension: either a standard design, perhaps with an extra room on top if your house has more than one storey, or something more exotic, like a heavily glazed, conservatory-like structure. Whatever it looks like, an extension has the advantage of taking up a comparatively small area of your garden.

Home workers with land to spare, however, might consider erecting a completely separate structure to work in. This solution, although potentially expensive, offers most in terms of space, quiet, privacy and psychological separateness – the feeling of entering and leaving a dedicated work place. At its most basic, this structure could be a glorified shed with power laid on; at the other extreme, it could be a substantial outbuilding, integrated visually with house and garden, and equipped with a full complement of services – electricity, telecommunications, plumbing and drainage. With the addition of a small shower room and sleeping facilities, a solidly constructed work annexe can even do double duty as guest quarters.

■ *Tucked under the eaves, with light flooding in on either side, this compact work area contains a fitted surface that makes the best possible use of space. Sleek black filing boxes are stacked to fit neatly under the angle of the roof.*

■ *Most separate work-space buildings have a modular structure that's easy to assemble and doesn't require planning permission. The simplest and cheapest designs are intended only as offices or studios, while the most sophisticated have fully fitted kitchens and bathrooms, making them suitable for use as either a permanent live/work unit or a luxurious office and occasional guest annexe.*

If you are drawn to the idea of a self-contained office that meets your exact specifications, start by talking through your requirements and tastes with an experienced architect, who will guide you through the necessary planning and construction processes. Or, if you're willing to compromise slightly on the personal service, investigate the possibility of an up-market, pre-fabricated building. These off-the-peg structures tend to be neatly designed, with pitched roof, proper windows and integral wiring and heating systems – some even have their own plumbing facilities. If you can find a design that suits your needs, you could be happily settled inside within a few days of delivery, and for about the price of a modest family car.

The box office

Detailed planning, custom-made fittings and close attention to detail transformed the tiny (three metres by two) box room in this Victorian terraced house into a stylish and hard-working home office. To accommodate a vast library of reference material for the garden designer and home economist who works here, one wall is almost completely filled by a huge old cupboard and the bookshelves made to fit on top of it; a clear illustration of the principle that oversized furniture can often make the very best use of a small space.

Facing this unit, and supported by two specially designed filing cabinets, is a curvy work surface cut from timber-faced blockboard to fit the room, and its function, precisely. Above the desk, spanning the length of the wall, a strong shelf is supported by metal brackets that add a decorative flourish.

The colour treatment involves a subtle brushwork effect on the pale walls, cool blue paintwork for the shelves and cupboard, and lots of natural wood and satin-finished metal.

■ *Fixed to the cupboard door panels (left), reclaimed roof slates act as mini blackboards.*

■ *Another witty yet very practical touch is provided by the galvanized metal wall unit, whose stylish, envelope-sized pockets were originally intended for seedlings. Note the functional (and coordinating) desk lamp (right).*

■ *Sturdy shutters help to filter out strong sunlight, reduce glare on the screen and provide added security (below).*

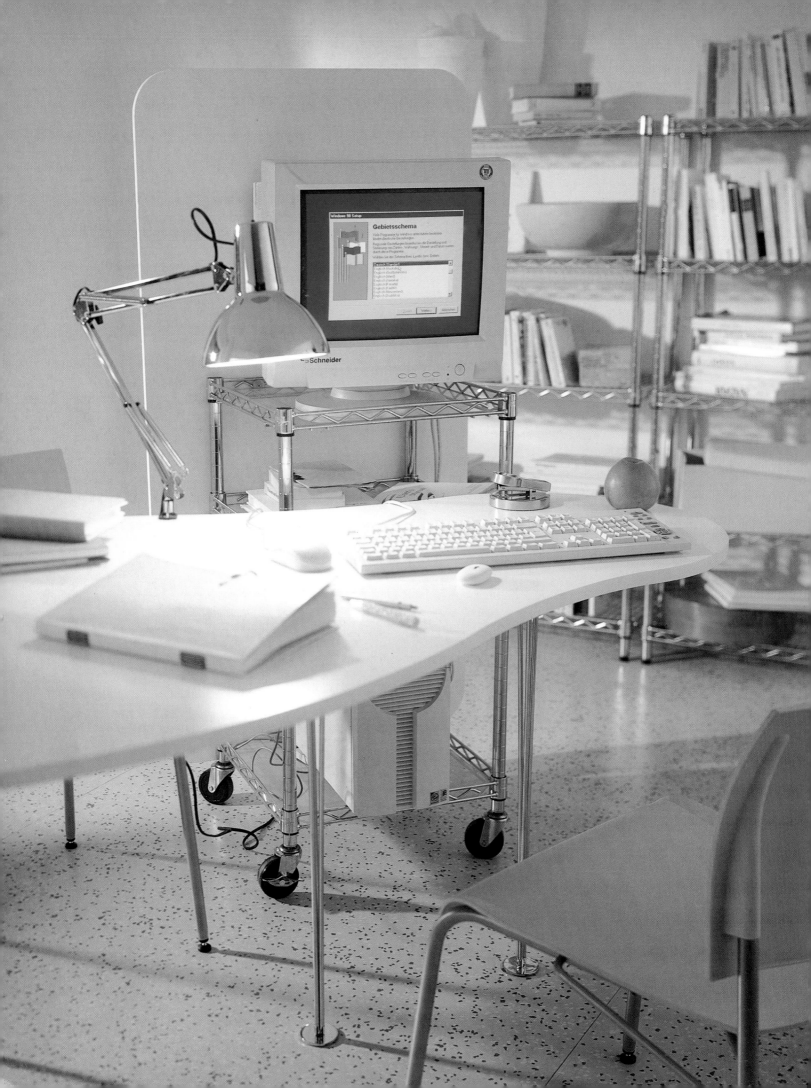

PART TWO

The practical elements

B ecause a home office is often tucked away out of sight, and tends to be associated with responsibility and toil rather than pleasure and relaxation, there is often a temptation to use it as a dumping ground for surplus furniture and equipment. Even those who take great pride in the decoration of the rest of their home are often happy to put a small, flimsy table and an extra dining chair in a gloomy corner and settle down to an extended session of paperwork.

The discomfort and disinclination to return that inevitably result are completely avoidable, however, since creating an efficient, well-equipped and ergonomically sound work space need not involve a great upheaval or a massive drain on finances. The key is to establish which elements should fulfil precise specifications and which can be improvised or adapted.

The chrome shelving units and trolley that provide all the storage in this work space can take very heavy loads, since they were originally intended for industrial use. They can also be assembled in whatever shape and size you need.

"ENTHUSIASM FINDS THE OPPORTUNITIES AND ENERGY MAKES THE MOST OF THEM."
HENRY HOSKINS

Furnishing schemes

The basic elements of all work spaces are the same: a surface to work at, a chair to sit on, provision for storage, appropriate lighting, and whatever special equipment or tools that are required for the job in hand.

A work surface can be as elaborate and expensive or as cheap and cheerful as you want. You certainly don't need a proper desk – a sturdy table, as long as it's the right size and height to suit both you and your tasks, will do perfectly well. Storage, too, can take the form of designer furniture, improvised bits and pieces or DIY shelving – just make sure that there's enough of it and that the contents are easy to get at when you need them.

Unless the time you plan to spend there is very limited indeed, however, don't attempt to furnish your home office with makeshift seating or lighting: a purpose-designed chair and good illumination are absolutely essential for the sake of your physical well-being and your day-to-day comfort.

When you set off in search of the items you need, don't limit your explorations exclusively to shops that sell only domestic or commercial furniture. Architectural salvage companies, and often larger stores that deal

■ *From the huge range of home-office furniture that has flooded the market in recent years, the owners of this home have chosen a small freestanding desk that fits into the tiny triangle under the stairs (above). When a fully equipped office has to slot into a restricted space, however, installing a fitted work station is often the wisest approach (left).*

■ *Order and calm preside in this work area situated on a top landing, where nothing is allowed to detract from the overwhelming impression of space and light: unobtrusive blinds almost disappear to let the sunlight in; the balustrade is transparent; and the desk top consists of a single sheet of thick glass (opposite).*

■ *In this cheerful live/work space (opposite), a colourful screen hanging from the ceiling helps to partition off the office from the rest of the room. When the whole floor area is needed for entertaining, the screen comes down and the desk rolls away on its heavy-duty castors.*

in second-hand furniture, also carry wonderful fittings that have been ripped out of old shops and schools: things like glass-fronted display cupboards, storage chests, drawer units and lockers as well as conventional items like desks and chairs. Other possible hunting grounds for unusual and practical office furniture are catering and hospital supply firms, where you can find similarly useful storage pieces as well as large, strong trolleys and tables.

The other furnishing element that should be chosen with practical considerations firmly in mind is the floor covering. Hard floors wear well and are easy to clean, but tend to be cold and unyielding underfoot and potentially noisy, both for you and for those in the rooms nearby. Carpet is more comfortable to walk on and offers both heat and sound insulation; for an office, the range you choose should have a durable (ideally contract-quality) flat-pile construction, especially if the castors of your chair will be skating back and forth constantly over one small area. The other advantage of flat-pile floor coverings (and hard floors, too, of course) is that, in a room full of electrical equipment, they don't produce the irritating static that makes your hair stand on end and your clothes cling to the back of your thighs.

■ *The ordered simplicity of this tiny corner office is a result of clever planning and design. The wall-fixed fitted desk makes excellent use of the space and leaves the floor clear. Painted to match the storage unit, the desk has a graphic triangular shape that is echoed in both the chair back and the subtle change of floor covering that sets the work area off from the rest of the room (right).*

Work surfaces

Until fairly recently, there were essentially only two main options when it came to a work surface: a freestanding desk or table, or a fitted work top. In the last few years, however, a third alternative has appeared: the sophisticated, purpose-designed computer unit.

Traditional commercial desks can range from fantastically elaborate L- or U-shaped designs with storage pedestals, surfaces of different heights for writing and keyboard work (either fixed or adjustable), slide-away extensions and privacy screens, to the most rudimentary versions that look like small dining tables. Some people would be lost without integral drawers, while others prefer a drawerless desk, and keep their accoutrements in a separate pedestal with a specially selected configuration of drawers – deep,

■ *Smooth white laminate covers this deep, uncluttered expanse of fitted surface that accommodates two work stations, yet blends discreetly with the bare white walls to concentrate all visual interest on the spectacular views (right).*

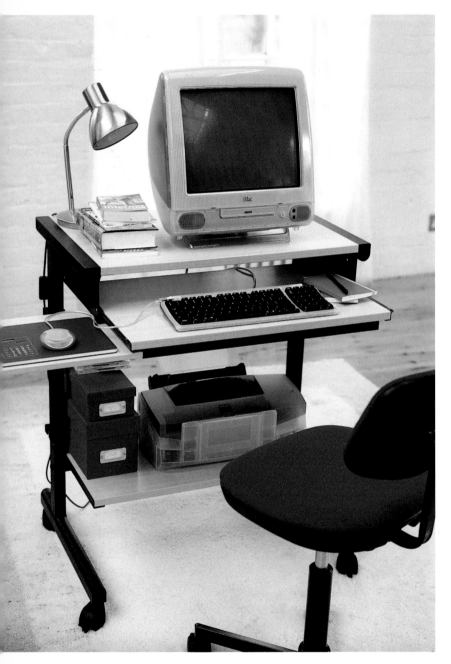

■ *Specialized computer units are not only easy to move around, they are much less obtrusive than conventional desks or tables, and usually come in a choice of colours and finishes.*

shallow or filing sizes. Most pedestal units are on castors, so they can tuck neatly under the desk or be pulled out to provide additional surface space.

Pedestals like these are the secret to transforming an ordinary kitchen, dining or trestle table into an efficient work surface instantly. Remember, however, that real desks are the right height for most people to work at (about 75cm/30in), or at least close enough so that an adjustable office chair can compensate for any slight discrepancies. So before you settle on a table intended for a different purpose, it's important that you try it out to make sure it isn't wildly too high or too low.

Installing a built-in desk, of course, means that you have control over choosing the size and shape of its surface and can fix it at whatever height is most comfortable for you. In addition, this alternative often makes the best use of limited space by extending right across the width of a box room, or even one of its corners. Apart from fitting exactly, a built-in surface is space-efficient because it doesn't have legs to get in the way of a radiator or a chunky skirting board. The downside of having a built-in work surface is that rearranging or relocating your work area involves much more effort.

FLEXIBLE FURNITURE

The latest addition to the market, dedicated computer desks were originally conceived to appeal to home workers. Sleekly designed in a variety of tough finishes and bright colours, these work stations are available in several sizes and ergonomically inspired shapes to suit every domestic location, from a tiny alcove to the corner of a sizable room.

Computer desks also offer maximum flexibility – not only in use, but also in location, since they are fairly easy to shift from one room to another. Some models have an adjustable-height work surface that whizzes up and down electronically so that you can work standing up, sitting down or perching on a stool. Most of these units feature an integral cabling channel that houses

wires neatly and safely, special shelves to accommodate such things as the CPU, printer, scanner, telephone and fax, and a range of optional extras for storing paraphernalia such as floppy disks and CDs.

Interestingly, the efficiency and style offered by the best computer desks have made them increasingly popular with large businesses as well as home workers, particularly those who have discovered that staff are significantly more productive in a bright, cheerful office than a grey, impersonal one.

■ *The ultimate luxury is a work surface that accommodates not just a desk area but also enough additional space for two or more projects-in-progress to be laid out simultaneously.*

■ *With a laptop you can easily set up office on different surfaces such as this long, narrow counter set into a wide arch cut through a partition wall (opposite).*

■ *Domestic desks from every style, period and design discipline fulfil their function in ingenious ways. A neoclassical secretaire (top left) conceals small shelves and drawers behind a hinged panel that flaps down to form the writing surface. An Art* *Deco desk (above left) curves out on either side of the central drawer to accommodate deep storage pedestals. A custom-built computer cabinet features a sliding keyboard drawer, a channel for the cabling and compartments for accessories (above right).*

Chairs and seating

For anyone who spends more than snatched moments seated at a desk or computer station, the most important item of furniture is undoubtedly the main work or task chair. This reality is not immediately obvious in the same way as, say, the inconvenience and muddle that result from an inadequate work surface or shelving system, because you can perch on a totally inappropriate chair for quite a while before you begin to feel really uncomfortable. It's not until you try to get up and walk that the full extent of your creakiness becomes apparent. Relied on over a period of weeks or months, the wrong chair can leave you constantly tired and headachy, prevent you from concentrating fully and cause permanent damage to your back, neck and shoulders.

■ *For use at a drawing board, choose an adjustable drafting chair (above). If you spend long hours at a conventional desk, invest in a good purpose-designed model (below and right).*

PERFECT POSTURE

A good, purpose-designed work chair is smoothly padded all over, with a seat that adjusts in height and, ideally, in angle as well. The chair's back should also move up and down, and tilt to support your spine when you lean forward or back or sit upright, so that good posture feels easy and natural and you aren't tempted to collapse into an unhealthy and unattractive slump. The back should also be shaped to give extra support to your low back (lumbar spine), which is especially vulnerable to strain and injury. A few models are made with a separate lumbar support that adjusts up or down to suit the height of the occupant. Another option for those with low-back problems is working on a kneeler chair, which directs most of the body's weight so that it isn't pressing down on the base of the spine.

■ *Some task chairs are bound to suit you better than others, so try out as many as possible before you buy. This sleek black model does all the right tricks and matches the style of the room (opposite).*

For maximum comfort, many people prefer a chair with armrests (padded or not); here again, these should be adjustable so that, whatever your proportions, you can sit with your forearms parallel to the floor. It's worth bearing in mind that armrests may prevent your chair from tucking neatly under your work surface when it's not in use.

Make sure that your chair is stable. Most office models are set on five legs that radiate out from a central pedestal; older versions sometimes have only four legs, but this construction is more vulnerable to overbalancing when you reach or lean too far in one direction. For ease of movement, your chair should be fitted with smooth-running castors that will whizz you noiselessly around your work area, and a swivel mechanism that enables you to change direction without having to shift your chair or twist your body.

To enhance the comfort and support provided by an existing office chair, try adding a small cylindrical cushion known as a lumbar roll, which you strap on to the frame so that it fits in the small of your back.

■ Your main task chair should have an adjustable seat and back, and should balance firmly on five legs; castors make it easy to move around (right). To soften and personalize the utilitarian look of a standard office chair, cover the seat and back with simple slipcovers (far right).

Another worthwhile extra is a wedge-shaped seat pad that works in the same way as a forward-tilting seat to encourage a healthier posture; some wedge cushions have a cut-out section under the base of the spine to relieve the pressure there.

Designers, architects and anyone who spends time at a drawing board should invest in a drafting chair. Similar to conventional task chairs, these provide support in the same way but are considerably higher and often feature an integral footrest.

EXTRA SEATING

If your work space is not in your living room, it is worth accommodating a proper upholstered or easy chair with its own reading light nearby to offer a welcome change of pace to the working day. When you are faced with a pile of things to read or when you need to make a series of long telephone calls, you can take the opportunity to change your position and so help to relieve muscle strain and stiffness.

■ When your desk is intended only for occasional use, you can allow style rather than ergonomics to dictate your choice to a greater extent (below and below left).

Your choice of guest seating should be geared to the number of people you are expecting and, more importantly, the length of time they are likely to stay. Visitors who pop in to leave or collect work will appreciate somewhere to sit, but a simple folding or stacking chair will do. Regular meetings with clients or colleagues, however, will be much more pleasant – and more productive – if there are enough comfortable chairs to go around. If you have to store them in another room when they're not in use, look for lightweight designs – perhaps in wicker or cane – and provide plump seat and back cushions.

■ *Classic folding chairs provide valuable extra seating for visitors and take up very little space (above). To keep the floor area clear, store them in their own wall rack, or hang them individually on wall-mounted hooks.*

■ *High-backed task chairs offer considerable extra support in the neck and shoulder area, where many people experience tension and stiffness (left).*

■ *With their padded leather seats and backs, these simple, modern armchairs are ideal for business meetings yet work equally well in a domestic setting.*

TAKE A BREAK

No matter how well your chair is designed and made, you should avoid sitting in one position for regular, extended periods. To avoid stiffness, tension and strain on your shoulders and back (and your eyes), get up every hour or so, walk around for a few minutes, stretch your legs, arms and fingers, and relax. In a conventional office environment there is always a certain amount of natural activity and human interaction, so it is particularly important for people working alone at home to develop the habit of taking regular breaks.

When the pressure begins to build, remember that you'll think more clearly and work more efficiently if you take time out to clear your mind and relax your body. The occupant of this home office can enjoy a stroll in the garden or stretch out on the sofa with a favourite magazine.

Lighting

■ *Wherever your office is situated, appropriate lighting is vital for both your productivity and your health. For use on a traditional desk, make your choice from the wide range of classic and modern designs available (right). Alternatively, explore less conventional arrangements, such as Philippe Starck's 'working bed', which comes complete with task lamps as well as computer shelf, power points and cabling channels (opposite).*

When a room simply doesn't work for you, and you never feel happy or comfortable there, your first impulse might be to change the colour scheme or replace the furniture or the curtains. In a surprising number of cases, however, the lighting is at fault. Wherever you're setting up your work area, therefore, check first of all to see if the main source of light is a central ceiling or pendant fitting. These do not provide enough light to work by, and their weak, widely spread illumination is deeply unflattering. Also, the position of a central light makes it more likely to be reflected in your computer screen, so you should consider either getting rid of the light altogether, or using it only in emergencies.

In working spaces, as in all other rooms, there are two main types of lighting: task lighting, which is fairly strong and aimed directly at your work, and background, or ambient, lighting, which is much more subtle and designed to illuminate the rest of the room. Ambient light should also eliminate harsh contrasts between the light on your work surface and the area around it. At night, background lighting has to be provided artificially, but during working hours, daylight, skilfully controlled, can perform this function very well.

CALM WORKING SPACES

"LIGHT IS A PRINCIPAL BEAUTY
IN A BUILDING."

THOMAS FULLER

■ When it comes to illumination, the work space in this New York loft has all the bases covered: on the desk, a treble-armed task lamp offers maximum brightness and flexibility in sculptural form, while the huge skylight window and adjoining terrace provide natural ambient lighting during office hours. At night, a row of modern pendant fittings and a curvy table model take over this function.

68

TASK LIGHTING

■ *However restricted your work space or traditional your decorating style, you should have no trouble finding a task lamp that provides appropriate illumination and blends harmoniously with its surroundings.*

Along with a good chair, a strong, clear light source is one of the essential elements of any work station; install an inadequate or inappropriate lighting system and you risk a variety of problems that will threaten your health and impair productivity, such as eye-strain, headaches, dizziness, back and neck pain, and exhaustion.

When the most time-consuming paperwork you undertake is a letter or a pile of bills, you might get away with a spare table lamp, but for any serious clerical or computer work, you need a model that is specially designed for the job. This will still hold true when you work directly in front of a window, since you'll still need to supply efficient task lighting on gloomy days and when night falls. The best task lighting is adjustable – at least in direction (so it can swivel towards a desk or a computer screen) and occasionally in intensity as well. Two of the

most popular choices are the classic Anglepoise and traditional goose-neck designs, both of which are available with a weighted base or a clamp that fixes on to the edge of a nearby shelf – a valuable facility when space is tight. Standard spotlights (table, clamp and wall-fixed versions) and many modern desk lamps work on the same principle and offer varying degrees of flexibility and sophistication.

Whichever design you choose, situate it on (or above) the opposite side of your desk from the hand you normally write with in order to avoid working in your own shadow. Make sure that when the beam falls on your main work area, it doesn't cause glare on the screen of a nearby computer.

Your task lamp should take a bulb that produces light of at least 60-watt intensity. Remember, though, that an overly powerful beam can put as much strain on your eyes as one that is too weak; you may have to experiment to find the strength that best suits your work and your age. (The eyes of a 40 year old need three times more light to see as clearly as those of a 10 year old; at age 60, fifteen times more light is needed.) Be careful, too, to avoid a bare bulb (or even part of a bulb), or one that has even the faintest degree of flicker, both of which can cause serious discomfort.

If there is a shelf directly above your work surface, try fixing a fluorescent strip underneath the front edge, concealing it behind a deep edging strip. While lacking the flexibility of an adjustable desk lamp, this arrangement does offer a way of freeing up the maximum surface area when space is at a premium or when the stripped-down style of a modern desk lamp threatens to jar with a period decorating scheme.

LIGHT EFFECTS

There are three main types of light.

■ **TUNGSTEN LIGHT** is the type produced by conventional household bulbs; it gives a slightly warm colour cast to everything it illuminates. Tungsten bulbs are fairly inexpensive, but they need to be replaced frequently and they produce a considerable amount of heat in use.

■ **FLUORESCENT LIGHT** usually emanates from ceiling-fixed tubes. These last much longer, use less energy and remain cooler to the touch than tungsten bulbs. They cast a cold light, however, which many people find harsh and unflattering.

■ **HALOGEN LIGHT** is produced by bulbs that are much smaller than either of the alternatives. The light is strong, clear and natural (without a warm or cool cast) – an important consideration when colour figures largely in your work. Although halogen bulbs are the most expensive, they have a long working life; this, together with their compact size, strength and clarity, makes them a popular choice for sleek designer lighting.

■ *To harmonize with the nautical atmosphere of this peaceful study and the mellow glow of its oak panelling, a brass desk lamp in a classic goose-neck shape is the perfect choice.*

■ *Installing a selection of different light sources will pay dividends in terms of your long-term comfort and productivity. In this multi-function room, an Anglepoise can be adjusted to focus powerful light on the desk or the couch, while halogen spotlights and a large, elegant table lamp provide valuable background illumination.*

A row of recessed ceiling spots illuminates the library shelves that line this study, and provides gentle background lighting at the same time (right).

BACKGROUND LIGHTING

Once you've sorted out an efficient task light for your work area, supplement it with soft background, or ambient, lighting of some description. If your desk is in a bedroom or living room, the existing fixtures – table, floor or wall lights, recessed ceiling fixtures or flexible track systems – should provide just the right amount of illumination. When maximum flexibility is a priority, fit dimmer switches so that you can adjust the level of lighting to suit a range of different activities.

If you have a separate work room, choose one or more background lights that will suit your chosen style and the space available. Maybe a quirky or eccentric design that caught your eye but could not meet the stringent requirements of a task light could be used in a supporting role. Where there is limited surface space, look for wall fixtures or neat, track-mounted spots instead of table lights. Or think about concealed lighting – perhaps tucked under a run of shelves or at the back of a deep picture rail.

Some lamps are versatile enough to serve as both task and background lights. An adjustable spot or a lamp with a jointed construction, for example, can be angled towards your desk to illuminate your work and focus your concentration. Then, when it's time to relax, you can turn it to highlight a nearby plant or picture, or simply to cast a warm glow on the ceiling or the wall.

Supplying subtle ambient light are a giant, cone-shaped floor lamp and a huge, rectangular uplighter suspended from the ceiling (below).

If you work beside a large window, hang a curtain or blind that pulls easily into place to protect your eyes from glare. Semi-opaque window treatments will help to filter out sunlight without throwing the room into gloom. Remember, too, to make adequate provision for grey, rainy days in the form of good task lighting (right and opposite).

In a high-ceilinged studio, sunlight floods in through the overhead skylight, creating a decorative pattern of silhouettes on the pale timber floor (above).

DAYLIGHT

Asked to describe their ideal work space, most people would probably think first of words like 'bright' and 'sunny'. This is not surprising, since as well as contributing to the general level of illumination, streaming sunlight has the power to transform even the least prepossessing room and to lift the spirits of its occupants.

In your haste to position your desk as near to a window as possible, though, remember that daylight can create problems of its own. A computer screen that faces a window, for instance, is vulnerable to glare. In the same way, positioning your desk so that you look directly out of a large or sunny window forces you to stare into light that is much too strong to be comfortable or healthy for your eyes. The best position for a computer (or a desk) is at right angles to a window, so that light falls on your working area without reflecting off a screen or straining your eyesight.

When it comes to window treatments, one of the best options is a blind or a pair of shutters with slats or louvres that can be adjusted to angle the light on your desk when you need it, or to direct it up or down when the sun shines too brightly. Venetian blinds fulfil this function perfectly: they're reasonably inexpensive, they can be custom made to fit your window, and they are available in a variety of materials including metal, plastic and wood. Vertical louvre blinds work on the same principle, but their somewhat institutional appearance rules them out of some traditional design schemes. Wooden shutters, on the other hand, may not blend easily with a modern, pared-down look, but they have a simple, natural appeal and a strong advantage when it comes to security.

If you prefer a softer look, choose curtains or roller blinds in a low-key style that reflects the room's professional function, yet makes it more appealing and personal. As a finishing touch, simple net curtains, or even panes of frosted glass, will preserve your privacy while admitting a gentle, diffused light.

Storage solutions

Equipping your work place with a well-planned storage system – one that provides not only enough storage space but also the right kind – will help you to operate more efficiently and so encourage a calm and orderly atmosphere. Whatever storage provision you decide on, try to make it flexible enough to cope with any increase or change in your work and with the inevitable accumulation of paperwork and possessions over time.

OFFICE INVENTORY

Begin by making a rough list of the items you need to accommodate: books, perhaps, leaflets and manuals, correspondence files, sales records, drawing materials or samples. Jot down a brief description and quantity in each case and, where appropriate, what kind of access you need. You might, for example, have five or six reference books that deserve a place beside your desk, since you use them all the time, several dozen more that are consulted regularly enough to warrant space on a nearby shelf, and a small number of obscure volumes that you look at so rarely they could happily live in another room.

Similarly, you may refer constantly to a particular category of document – current contracts, maybe, or outstanding orders – so they should stay within reach; less active records can be cleared out regularly and moved to a high shelf or a cupboard. (And even apart from considerations of space, an overflowing file is clumsy and awkward to use.) What about stationery? If buying in bulk makes sense in terms of price or convenience, you will have to find a place for it.

SHELVING

In commercial, as well as domestic, life, a generous run of shelves, freestanding or fitted, can cope with a great many storage requirements. Freestanding shelves come in a huge range of prices and styles; they can be moved around easily and even those that require self-assembly are fairly straightforward to put up. Built-in shelves can be adapted to suit your needs precisely and they make the best use of space – both by filling the

■ *Available in a range of sizes, neat storage boxes will swallow up all kinds of office material, from dead files to stationery.*

■ *Modular storage units keep a variety of items neat and organized; note the shelves built into the cupboard door. A large plan chest below provides additional storage.*

available area (an alcove or even a wall) completely, and, if you vary their height, by containing an assortment of different-sized items in compartments that fit them exactly. Once they are in place, however, fitted shelves are much more trouble to dismantle if you decide to move home, or even just to re-locate your office to another room. If the shelves are too flimsy or badly made, they also have a tendency to look cheap and untidy. When you're planning or building a run of shelves, therefore, remember that

books and papers are very heavy, so use thick board and provide plenty of supports.

Box and ring files, storage cases, folders, stationery and much more can also be swallowed up by a sturdy shelving system, but remember that not all office paraphernalia has the same visual appeal as books, so consider providing closed cupboards of some description – again, either fitted or freestanding. For bulky storage, set aside a deep filing drawer, or see if you can adapt an item of domestic furniture such as a large chest of drawers, perhaps, a wardrobe with added shelves, a lidded trunk, chest or blanket box, or a graceful linen press or armoire.

■ *To store books and files within easy reach, choose a revolving bookcase (ancestor of the designer trolley) (left) or a small shelf unit on castors (left above).*

"NO FURNITURE SO CHARMING
AS BOOKS."

SYDNEY SMITH

■ *To cater for all your storage
requirements, combine a wall of carefully
planned fitted shelves (left) with a chunky
freestanding unit that you can wheel from
place to place (below).*

The most ingenious storage solutions are not necessarily modern and hi tech. With its rows of compartments, this exquisite 17th-century Italian legal cabinet makes an eye-catching filing system.

MASTERING THE PAPERWORK

The type of system you choose for storing and organizing paperwork will depend on how much of it you intend to process, and how complicated it is. Something like a ring binder, for example, is ideal for simple correspondence; index tabs will divide it alphabetically or into categories if necessary, and you can keep the whole file on or near your desk. Once you begin receiving, or generating, large amounts of paper of any kind, you may need to invest in a proper filing cabinet with two or four drawers, or a combination of these. Taller models take up less floor area, but the shorter ones provide more useful surfaces – bridged with a sheet of MDF (medium-density fibreboard), two of them can form a desk.

■ *A tiny corner cupboard has been turned into a useful storage area for home-office supplies. Wall-mounted magazine racks keep papers in check and a pinboard has been attached to the back of the door. An adjustable spotlight illuminates the space without getting in the way (above).*

■ *Constructed on the same principle as an old-fashioned steamer trunk, this mobile office box has two hinged sections fitted out with drawers and shelves as well as an extending work surface (left).*

■ *Instead of piling maps, plans and drawings on top of one another, roll them up neatly, label them clearly and store them in a tall bin (below).*

■ *Wire filing trays slotted into a three-tiered shelf unit help to keep the desk free of clutter and provide an extra surface on top (above).*

If you deal frequently with outsize papers such as charts, proofs, technical drawings or maps, see if you can fit a designers' plan chest into your work space. Fitted with varying numbers of large, shallow drawers, these, like low filing cabinets, provide lots of useful surface space as a bonus. To store giant bits of paper on a smaller scale, roll them up and stick them in a large cylindrical bin – a laundry or waste-paper basket perhaps. Or tuck each one into a pair of large hooks fixed side by side on a spare patch of wall. Actually, a clear wall can support storage facilities of several different kinds: a strong pinboard, a grid system with hooks, a plastic or metal wall pocket, or a wire magazine rack to hold wallet folders where they are easy to see and reach.

If your working space shares its quarters with the living or dining room, you might find it useful to keep your equipment and material on a big trolley. When you are working, you can wheel it into position near your desk; to clear the space at the end of the day, you can easily tuck it under a table or in a cupboard, or push it into another room.

Equipment and technology

■ *Clear your work surface by standing your VDU on an adjustable platform attached to an extending swivel arm. This model has an integral chrome handle that also serves as a retractable keyboard tray.*

The fantastic advances in modern technology in recent years have enabled more and more people to receive and send information from their computer, and as access to the Internet, e-mail and other on-line services increases, home working will get easier and more popular. At the same time, personal computers continue to grow in power and performance yet shrink in size and cost. With such an array of rapidly developing technology, however, making the right choice can seem bewildering. Unless you are knowledgeable and confident enough to research the market and identify exactly what you need,

■ *Choose the computer and accessories best suited to the job you do, then look around for the most efficient and good-looking furniture you can afford to house* *them. In this sunny corner, a compact work station, a coordinating pedestal storage unit and two handy windowsills accommodate all the necessary equipment.*

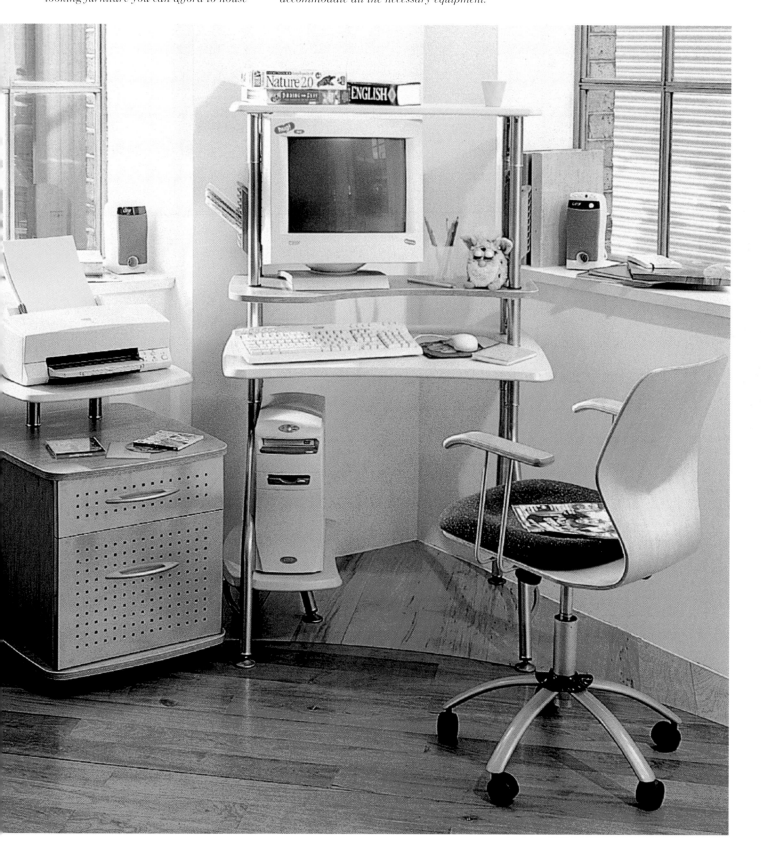

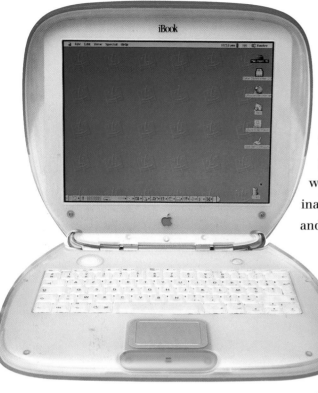

■ *Labelling the connections on your computer and other pieces of equipment will ensure that you don't accidentally pull out the wrong plug (opposite).*

seek advice from someone who is familiar both with computer technology in general and the requirements of your business in particular. A computer represents a serious financial investment, and, whatever magic they can perform in the right circumstances, an inappropriate or uninformed choice has the capacity to inspire profound and crippling frustration.

As well as meeting the specialist needs of your job, your system should be comfortable to use. Look particularly for an adjustable VDU (visual display unit) that will tilt and swivel into the best position for you. If a certain amount of glare is unavoidable, fix a special shade to your screen to minimize the effect. Modern printers tend to be fairly quiet in use, but if yours isn't (or if you have an older daisy-wheel or dot-matrix model), tuck a foam mat underneath it to absorb the noise and vibration.

With any piece of equipment – computer, printer, fax machine, telephone, answering machine or photocopier (and combinations of these) – finding the most appropriate model is essentially a matter of identifying which features you need and which you are never likely to use,

■ *The appealing curves of this compact laptop have been specially contoured for ease of handling. Designed for maximum portability, the computer has an exceptionally strong case with no vulnerably protruding hardware – even the handle folds away completely (above).*

and taking decisions strictly on that basis. Making purchases instinctively, without assessing your technological needs, has a tendency to lead you in one of two directions, according to your personality. One possibility is that you will, on the 'just in case' principle, acquire the most sophisticated and complex models of every conceivable appliance and gadget on the market – an approach that is likely to be a waste of space and money (and could land you with technology that you find too intimidating to use).

■ *Specially strengthened drawers with extending runners allow bulky items of equipment to slide away smoothly when they are not in use (left).*

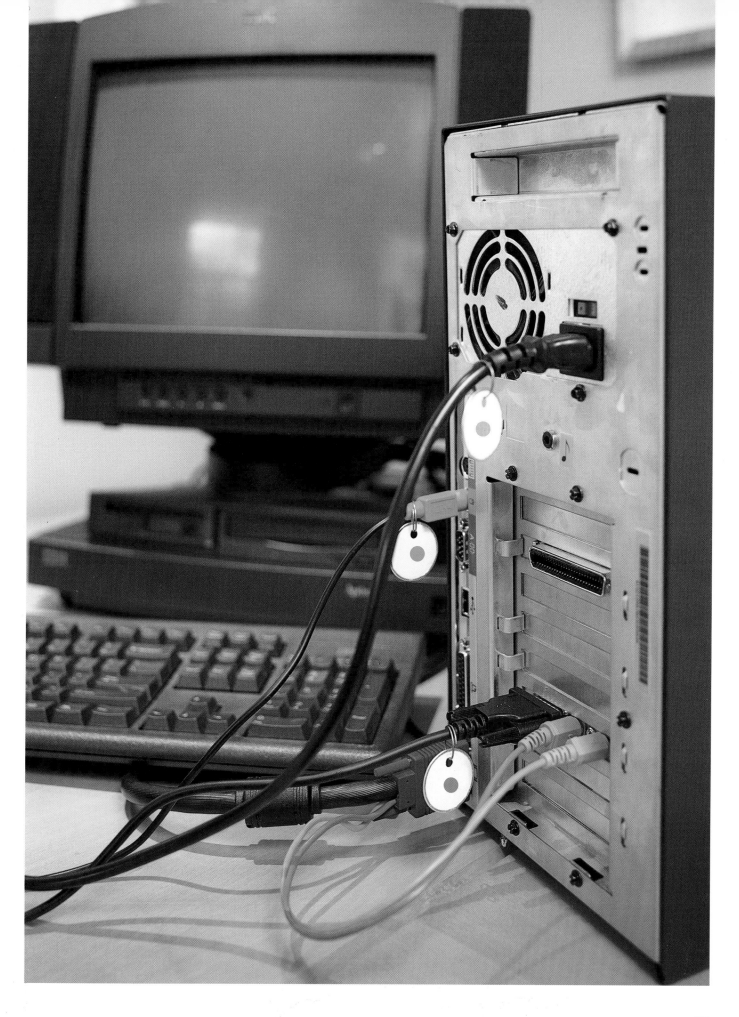

CALM WORKING SPACES

■ *An L-shaped work station with a*
separate computer extension allows your
main desk to be kept clear and provides a
slightly lower surface for your keyboard;
in addition, many models also feature
an integral platform for the central
processing unit (CPU).

The other danger is that you will try to keep costs down by making do with as few items of equipment as possible, and automatically choose the least expensive, most rudimentary design of each. This approach is equally misguided, when paying a little more might mean you gain a range of features that will ultimately save you time (and therefore money) and make your working life run more smoothly and efficiently.

So, for example, if you use your fax machine only occasionally, it would make sense to choose one that has an integral answering machine and perhaps a copier as well. If you send and receive a lot of faxes, however, you will need a separate, single-purpose machine. (And if you keep and file most of your documents, it's worth paying a little more for a model that uses individual sheets of plain paper, since faxes printed on coated, continuous-roll paper are not only less tidy looking, they also fade over a period of time.)

Similarly, investing in your own photocopier – even a compact desk model – might be highly cost (and time) effective if too many of your busy days are interrupted by trips to the nearest commercial machine.

■ You can take steps to counteract the long-term problems associated with sitting at a computer for long periods by investing in an ergonomic mouse and keyboard (this page). Home workers can now choose from a vast range of compact equipment that will function effectively and unobtrusively in even the smallest of working corners (opposite).

"THE NEW ELECTRONIC INTERDEPENDENCE RECREATES THE WORLD IN THE IMAGE OF A GLOBAL VILLAGE."
MARSHALL MCLUHAN

OPERATING SAFELY

If your work (or play) entails long hours at a computer, it is important to protect yourself against repetitive strain injury (RSI). This is largely caused by the slight but constant tension necessary for fingers to make the repeated, but very small, movements needed to operate hypersensitive keys without ever being able to rest on them.

Potential problems are exacerbated by an awkward angle between forearms and keyboard or hand and mouse, so investigate some of the ergonomic features and accessories designed with these dangers in mind: a wrist support and special mouse pad, perhaps, adjustable in height and angle and available as separate add-ons. Some conventional keyboards feature an integral wrist support, while others are moulded into curves that accommodate the shape of each hand perfectly and provide maximum support for palms and fingers as well as wrists.

Other recent innovations include task chairs and work surfaces with integral keyboard trays, and wrist and mouse pads designed for safety and comfort.

The design of the standard mouse is thought to contribute to some cases of repetitive strain injury, so if you are aware of any discomfort when you work, look for one with a different shape or operating mechanism intended to reduce the strain on the wrist and forearm.

■ *For maximum efficiency, try to organize your work space so that everything you use regularly is stored within a few steps of your desk (opposite). To keep the top of your work surface free from untidy paperwork, attach a clip-on wire filing basket to a nearby shelf (above).*

■ *If your desk has no integral drawers, a separate storage pedestal is bound to be useful. The most popular models have either three small drawers (right), or one small drawer and one deep one for hanging files. They tuck neatly under the desk or can be wheeled out to provide an additional surface.*

Working order

Once you've researched and acquired the right furnishings and equipment for your needs, the next step in creating your work space is deciding on its layout and organization.

When space is very tight, or you are commandeering part of an existing room, there tends to be a limited number of places that your desk or work surface will fit. Discovering the optimum position for all the furniture in a separate, dedicated office, however, is a more complicated proposition, so begin by drawing the room's exact shape on graph paper, indicating the position of such things as doors, windows, radiators and electrical sockets.

Experiment with possible floor plans by moving around on this drawing accurately scaled shapes cut out of card to represent the major items of furniture. Since your desk is probably the largest and most important of these, position this first, making sure it gets plenty of natural light (and the benefit of any available view) and allocating enough surrounding space for safe and convenient access (see pages 162–163).

Next, work out which items are used most frequently (a fax machine, perhaps, and a filing cabinet), and locate them in appropriate proximity to your desk. Even if you have to add extra storage facilities of some kind – like a trolley or more shelves – make sure that all the books and files you refer to constantly can be kept within easy reach of your work station. The time it takes to get up from your desk and walk across the room will, over time, add up to wasted hours. Again, for every item, whether free-standing or built-in, always allow enough space for convenient use and, where necessary, clearance.

"GOOD ORDER IS THE FOUNDATION OF ALL THINGS."
EDMUND BURKE

■ *A dividing screen will offer some privacy for two people sharing a work station, while a slide-away extension increases the available surface (below).*

THE SCIENCE OF COMFORT

Whether your office takes up a tiny corner, a large room or a separate building, its nerve centre is the work station itself, and the only way to make sure this area is safe and comfortable to use is by employing the principles of ergonomics – a term that simply describes the way people relate to the things and spaces around them.

Research has shown, for example, that the height for a writing surface should be about 63–76cm (25–30in), while a keyboard should be 5–6cm (2–2½in) lower. The key element here, however, is the position of your body as you work: your natural posture should be fairly upright – if your back is rounded or your shoulders hunched, your desk is probably too low. (One of the great advantages of a purpose-designed chair is that you can adjust its height to suit your own desk or work space.)

■ *Your keyboard should be positioned about 5–6cm (2–2½in) below the work surface. Look for purpose-designed desks that feature an extending keyboard drawer (below).*

Your keyboard and mouse should be positioned so that, in use, your forearms lie parallel to the floor in a straight line through your wrists. Your thighs, too, should be parallel with the floor, without being compressed by the edge of your chair or the underside of the work surface. If your feet don't sit flat on the ground, or if you are more comfortable when they are supported or braced, provide a foot rest of some kind, either freestanding or wall-mounted (some models are adjustable in both height and angle), or a small stool.

To avoid strain on your eyes as well as your neck, back and shoulders, position your computer monitor 46–61cm (18–24in) away and slightly below eye level. If your monitor is too low, try propping it up with old telephone directories or books, or, for something more aesthetic, position it on a painted plywood box. Those who include

■ *Some modern desks have adjustable legs, making them an ideal choice for those who are well above or below average height (above).*

Viewing distance 46–61cm (18–24in)

Monitor at eye level or slightly lower

Forearms and wrists parallel to the floor

Copy holder

Chair supports low back

Wrist rest

Thigh clearance

Desk height 58–71cm (23–28in)

Foot rest

■ *Accessories such as an adjustable copy holder (above) and a tilting foot rest (right) can make a significant difference to your overall safety and comfort over a period of time.*

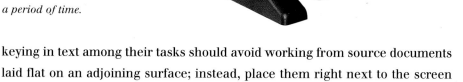

■ *If you are working from home full time, paying attention to the ergonomics of your work station will help you to maintain productivity and safeguard your health (above). Remember, though, that no matter how efficiently organized your work space, it is still imperative that you take regular breaks from your work (see page 65).*

keying in text among their tasks should avoid working from source documents laid flat on an adjoining surface; instead, place them right next to the screen in a document holder.

It's worth keeping in mind that the perils of a badly arranged work station often take time to reveal themselves, so if your keyboard is too high, your chair is not supporting your back, or your desk is too low, don't be lulled into believing the discrepancy doesn't matter. If you work there over long periods, day after day, your physical well-being (and your productivity) will suffer.

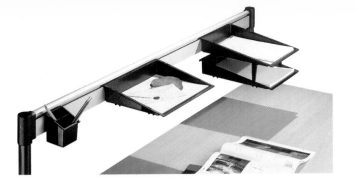

SURFACE ORGANIZATION

Although a badly laid out work surface is unlikely to cause physical problems, it can waste a lot of time and contribute to a general sense of confusion. To encourage order and efficiency, make sure all the items you use constantly such as the telephone, pens and pencils or note pad (and obviously your keyboard and mouse) are located where you can get at them without bending or stretching – that is within a radius of about 76cm (30in). Most people can reach just beyond this – between 76cm (30in) and 95cm (37½in) – if they do bend or stretch, so find a place within this arc for things you need fairly frequently. To touch anything beyond 95cm (37½in), you will probably have to stand up, so reserve the far reaches of your desk for objects you seldom touch.

Situate your telephone on the opposite side of your desk from your dominant hand (on your left if you're right-handed and vice versa) so that your writing hand stays free and the telephone flex is out of your way. To control paperwork, a set of filing trays is invaluable; most documents can be categorized under 'action', 'pending' or 'filing', and sorting each one according to this system as soon as it arrives will save you from having to plough through a heap of miscellanea every time you want to find something.

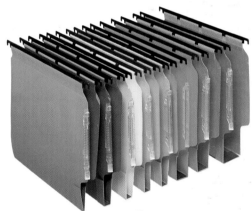

■ *If you find yourself constantly searching for bits of paper you've temporarily mislaid, keep all your work in progress in a set of hanging files close to your desk (above). Arrange pens, pencils and other office paraphernalia in a sliding tray that fits into the top drawer of your desk (top).*

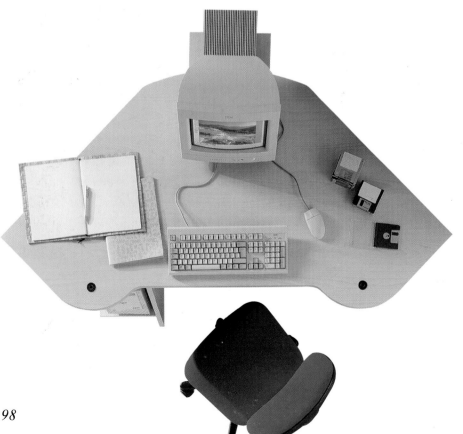

■ *This unusual corner work station provides a wide surface area within comfortable reach; at the far side, the narrow point of the triangle neatly accommodates the bulky back end of the VDU (left).*

■ *The gently curved shape of this sleek computer desk gives a softer, more organic look than conventional rectangular or square models; it also extends the surface* *area within easy access, while the arched legs leave maximum clearance underneath for the task chair. A hanging grid takes the place of a drawer for office supplies.*

Cabinet work

Fitting all the necessary elements of a home office (furniture, storage, equipment and wiring) into a corner of a living room or bedroom can be a challenge, and doing so without compromising the existing design scheme often proves to be impossible. One effective solution, however, is a purpose-designed, self-contained unit. Available in a range of styles to suit your home, and with doors that close to conceal the work in progress, these cabinets house all the equipment you need in a compact space.

■ *Lateral filing systems require less depth than those with a conventional frame. Arranging your files this way also allows you to see the entire contents of the drawer at a glance (left).*

■ *To reduce the risk of accidents and minimize visual clutter, all four doors slide neatly away into the frame when the work station is in use (right).*

■ *When the doors are closed, the unit looks like a traditional clothes press or armoire (left).*

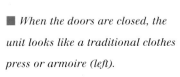

■ *Adjustable shelves, a sliding keyboard tray, special stationery compartments and a useful pinboard ensure that there is no wasted space inside this compact unit (left).*

■ *An integral holder allows the CPU to be pulled out and turned through 90 degrees to give easy access to the cabling (below).*

PART THREE

Working with style

Although the decoration of your home office might not be at the top of your list of priorities, the way it looks and the atmosphere it projects deserve just as much attention as any other part of your house. If you spend a large part of the day at your desk, creating an inspiring space that reflects your tastes is an important consideration.

An appealing, sympathetic scheme need not involve elaborate and costly furnishings and accessories. The simplest elements, used imaginatively, can often transform even the least prepossessing of corners into somewhere that instantly lifts the spirits, calms anxieties and mobilizes productivity – a work space so personal and stylish that the time you spend there is not an unwelcome interruption to your life but an integral and valued part of it.

■ *Cantilevered out from a dramatic concrete curve, a pale laminated surface provides the perfect spot for quiet contemplation beside a wall of library bookshelves in this New England house.*

"HAVE NOTHING IN YOUR HOUSES THAT YOU DO NOT KNOW TO BE USEFUL, OR BELIEVE TO BE BEAUTIFUL."

WILLIAM MORRIS

Choosing your style

■ *A rigid design discipline dominates this Art Deco inspired work space, where all the elements share a subtle geometric theme of elongated isosceles triangles – note the chair and desk legs, the ingenious slanting drawer and the pale wooden lamp base.*

Setting up a business from home – often on a self-employed basis – can be expensive and stressful, and your inclination might be to consign the aesthetics of your work space to the very bottom of your list of priorities. But we are all profoundly affected by our surroundings, and having an inviting, comfortable and personal environment in which to tussle with the pressures of the business world can make a significant difference to your state of mind and your success.

And bringing this about needn't be difficult or expensive; in many cases, good design choices cost no more than bad ones – it's just a matter of making the effort.

Of course, if you are planning to convert a corner of your living room or bedroom into a work place, these choices will be dictated largely by the existing decorations. The task (and the satisfaction) of creating a scheme from scratch comes into play only when you have a self-contained space with which to work.

BASIC PRINCIPLES

While you have everything to gain by making your work space appealing, this is not the place to experiment with your wildest decorating fantasies. Your surroundings should look organized and business-like, and they should be free of distractions to encourage calm, concentration and productivity. The rule here is to stay away from busy patterns, fussy details, trendy, multi-hued treatments and large areas of very strong colour altogether. (Even a monochrome scheme, if it's overpowering, can be unsettling to work in.)

For your own peace of mind, avoid furnishing your immediate work area with any items – large or small – that are

■ *A passion for painting, cinema, fashion and photography has provided the decorative influence in this feminine, light-filled Parisian apartment.*

■ *Classic 19th-century chairs are the only
stylistic link between the neutral-hued
studio of painter Peter Blake (left) and
architect Alistair Howe's cheerful
work area with its solid blocks of vivid
primary colour (below).*

especially valuable in either financial or sentimental terms. Instead, look for furniture and accessories sympathetic to the spirit of your scheme without being precious antiques or modern style icons. We all spill coffee and knock things over occasionally, and constant anxiety about an heirloom table or a designer light fitting is unlikely to foster an atmosphere of serenity.

A professional-looking office is especially important if clients or colleagues visit regularly – the setting in which they see you is bound to influence their impression of your competence. If you work in a creative field such as design or architecture there may be more scope for individuality than in more traditional ones like accounting, but, if your office is on display, make sure it reinforces the impression you want to give.

THE OVERALL PICTURE

Always bear in mind that all the areas in a house, flat or apartment should be linked visually in some way. This doesn't mean you're limited to the same style throughout, but try to avoid a clash of schemes that have nothing in common: a strongly architectural work space filled with state-of-the-art furniture and gadgets, for example, would sit uncomfortably in a home full of Victorian furniture and swagged curtains. Workable compromises here would be a subtler period scheme or modern furnishings in simple, elegant shapes and subdued colours, both of which would create a more professional impression than the Victorian opulence all around without looking out of place. If your work space is in a completely separate building, of course, your choices are less restricted.

A comfortable living area doubles up as commercial display space in this unusual domestic art gallery, run and owned by a couple who count painting, photography and graphic design among their talents. Notice how the spacious adjoining study blends seamlessly with the overall decorative style of the ground-floor rooms.

A STYLE FOR YOU

It's also important to make allowances for your own personality. If you are naturally ordered and neat, and find clear, open spaces calming, then a stark minimalist scheme would suit you perfectly. Those who are untidy, predisposed to hoarding or forced to function in a too-small space, however, would be foolish to attempt this design idiom, no matter how seductive it looks in glossy magazines. There's no getting away from the fact that architectural purity requires discipline to maintain, and struggling constantly to live up to your interior design will fray your nerves. (Remember, too, that this look requires considerable financial outlay to achieve in the first place – perfect surfaces and totally concealed facilities cannot be improvised.)

Often, too, mismatches between office and occupant occur on purely emotional grounds: if the rooms you feel happiest in are cosy and cluttered, then warm colours, open shelves and fitted carpet will create a more sympathetic environment for you than white walls, metal cupboards and studded rubber flooring. Of course, if your preference is for a clean, hard-edged look in all your rooms, it makes sense to treat your work space in the same way. But it's easy to develop an unnecessarily narrow view of what an office should look like. One of the great joys of working from home, after all, is exchanging the sterile functionality of the corporate environment for surroundings that are relaxing and personal.

FIT FOR THE PURPOSE

As well as being compatible with your personality, your work space should have a nodding acquaintance with the business that will be carried on there. Hi-tech furniture, industrial shelves and metal filing trays, for example, would not be a good choice for an interior designer whose potential clients are likely to favour flowery wallpaper and piles of cushions. By the same token, positioning yourself at the cutting edge of a creative or communications field might be tricky if you hold your meetings in an immaculately re-created 19th-century room.

■ *Another rustic look, this time in a small box room belonging to designer Sasha Waddell, where a pretty working corner has been tucked into an alcove. Pale walls, painted woodwork and fresh cotton fabrics all suggest Swedish country style.*

■ *The minimalist modern look of this dramatic loft work area throws all the visual emphasis on space, light and an inspiring natural view.*

IDEAS AND INSPIRATION

To kick start your imagination, look through as many specialist books and magazines as possible, and order a selection of catalogues from firms specializing in office or home-office equipment and furnishings. Increasingly, the boundaries between domestic and contract furnishing are being blurred. Not only do many consumer outlets carry at least one home-office range in their collection, but specialist firms who, only a few years ago, were interested only in dealing with large businesses, are producing purpose-designed, often scaled-down, furnishings intended for a domestic setting.

If anyone you know has a work space you particularly like, ask about the ideas behind it, and find out which features are successful and which have proved disappointing. Exposing yourself to lots of different ideas will help to define your taste. Also, when you examine a selection of rooms that appeal, the likelihood is that one look will dominate or that several common qualities – of colour, line or detail – will emerge that point you in the right direction. The secret of success is to make sure that the style of your work space encourages productivity while enhancing your feelings of well-being and comfort without being overpowering and distracting.

■ *In contrast, the charm of this very traditional study relies on furniture and accessories that reflect a bygone era: partners' desk, leather-bound desk accessories and a butler's tray that doubles up as storage space.*

Ancient wisdom

Feng shui, literally meaning wind and water, is an ancient Chinese discipline aimed at creating harmony through the selection and placement of the things around us. According to its principles, good feng shui harnesses and strengthens chi, a kind of energy or life force that affects everything about us – the way we look, the way we move, the way we behave and the way we feel, as well as our health, prosperity, personal fulfilment and destiny.

In practice, the Chinese art of placement, as feng shui is sometimes described, is about ensuring the flow of chi by removing or deflecting any object or force that acts as a block. This process of unblocking allows personal chi to connect with the chi in the environment, creating a oneness with nature that unlocks potential and encourages well-being and good fortune. In the East, feng shui masters are routinely consulted not only on the design, construction, decoration and furnishing of homes and offices but also on their location, their position on a particular site and even on the direction they face. Many multi-national corporations depend on these masters to guide every aspect of their property dealings. Although much of the wisdom is philosophical or mystical in nature, feng shui also involves a great deal of common sense, and has something to offer everyone who values order and harmony in their surroundings.

■ *Two very different work spaces share the auspicious qualities of visual calm and lofty openness that allow chi to flow freely. In addition, the traditional timber-clad studio (left) and the composed modern office (opposite) both have high, wide windows through which the vital force can enter and leave.*

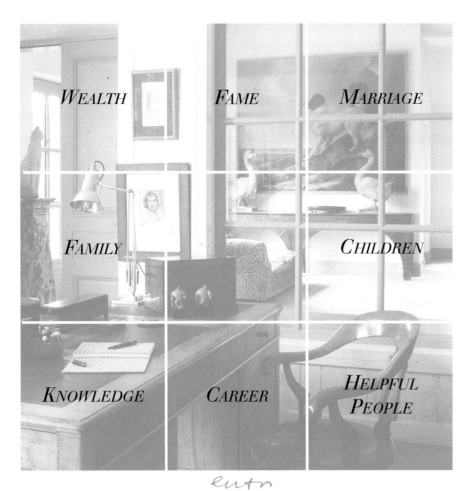

WEALTH   FAME   MARRIAGE

FAMILY   CHILDREN

KNOWLEDGE   CAREER   HELPFUL PEOPLE

■ *This chart, called the bagua, is used to divide rooms (and buildings) into eight sections corresponding with major aspects of life. This is done by superimposing the bagua on a plan of the room (or house) so that the entrance is on the bottom edge – in the Knowledge, Career or Helpful People square, according to its position; entrances on the Career and Helpful People squares are auspicious for business. The key areas in an office are: Career, Wealth, Fame and Helpful People, so ensure they are well-lit and free of interruptions to the flow of chi. For good fortune, install a water feature in one of them, and store anything related to money in the Wealth corner.*

STRUCTURED FOR SUCCESS

For those who have the luxury of choice when it comes to locating a separate work room, feng shui guidelines are specific: the proximity of any room to a building's main entrance directly reflects the importance of that room. The primary function of most homes is relaxation, which is why the living room tends to be close to the front door. If the work you do represents a full-time professional commitment, ensure a harmonious balance between work and relaxation by situating your office equally near the entrance. Try to avoid any room that opens off the end of a corridor, however, since the chi here will be channelled too intensely. When this is unavoidable, moderate its flow by hanging wind chimes in the doorway. Doors and windows are the vital portals through which chi enters and leaves a room, so make sure they all open freely and completely. Perfectly plain square or rectangular rooms with high ceilings are the most auspicious; low ceilings and exposed beams, for example, discourage the flow of chi and therefore sap energy and good fortune. To minimize this effect, paint low ceilings to match walls, and beams to blend with both (just one of the many ways in which feng shui lore dovetails neatly with sound decorating advice).

Other architectural features that create bad feng shui in a similar way are pillars or columns (especially when they are square rather than round) and projecting corners like those created by an L-shape or a chimney breast. In both cases, fix mirrors (in sheet rather than mosaic-tile form) on the outward-facing edges to attract positive chi, hang crystals in front of them to dilute and weaken bad chi, or soften their sharpness with trailing greenery. In feng shui, plants symbolize nature and encourage energy to flow, although prickly or spiky ones can shoot darts of bad fortune in all directions. Keep in mind though that all plants and flowers must be fresh and healthy: wilted or spindly specimens should be thrown away immediately.

■ *An entrance in the Career or Helpful People position bodes well for any goals that you are striving to achieve in your working life.*

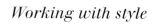

"A ROOM WITHOUT BOOKS IS A
BODY WITHOUT SOUL."
CICERO

■ *A flourishing, healthy plant will provide
a strong link with nature and encourage
energy and growth. The position of this
glossy-leaved Swiss cheese plant (*Monstera
deliciosa*) in the Wealth corner of a
beautifully proportioned and peaceful
room can only enhance its positive effect.*

117

Auspicious management

Feng shui principles of office design place primary importance on the position of the desk and set out a number of relevant strictures. Ideally, your desk should be situated diagonally opposite the door to establish control, concentration and authority. (A position too near the door, however, weakens your authority and your commitment to work.) There should be a solid wall behind your chair, but far enough away from it so that chi can circulate freely.

If at all possible, avoid sitting with your back to the door, since this makes you vulnerable to attack from behind in the form of betrayal or bad luck. Working under a beam or in front of a column is also discouraged, but the least desirable position of all for a desk is facing a wall – particularly if your back is to the door as well. In many small rooms, unfortunately, this arrangement utilizes the space most effectively; when this is the case, you can help to alleviate negative feng shui by placing a mirror in front of you that reflects the door, or hanging a picture of open countryside or an expanse of water there.

One of the basic tenets of feng shui is that rooms should be free of clutter, which plays havoc with the all-important flow of chi. The answer here is plenty of storage capacity designed for concealment rather than display. The most conventional way to achieve this is by investing in purpose-designed storage furniture, such as a large cupboard, a low

THE LANGUAGE OF COLOUR

Feng shui makes extensive use of colour, and ascribes particular associations to each one. Use these associations to choose an all-over scheme for your work space or to add splashes of colour to a particular area: a black stone in the Wealth corner, perhaps, or a red cushion in the Fame section.

 GREEN *represents tranquillity and is therefore an ideal choice for a working environment.*

 RED *denotes strength, positive energy and respect.*

WHITE *is the Chinese colour of mourning and can therefore have negative qualities, so substitute warm creams or other neutral shades.*

 YELLOW AND **ORANGE** *both have connotations of growth and confidence.*

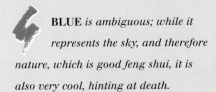 **GREY** *can encourage passivity and powerlessness if overused, but in smaller quantities its neutrality can balance an overly bright scheme.*

BLUE *is ambiguous; while it represents the sky, and therefore nature, which is good feng shui, it is also very cool, hinting at death.*

BLACK *is similarly equivocal. It suggests absence of light, so too much is a bad thing, but it is also the colour of money and income, making it an excellent choice for accents and accessories.*

chest or a filing cabinet, or by building in a generous shelf unit to which you can add ready-made doors or construct your own out of MDF (medium-density fibreboard). For a softer (and probably much cheaper) solution, disguise your shelves with floor-to-ceiling curtains in a plain, natural material, hung from a simple, slim pole sized along the top.

Steer clear of antique or second-hand items of furniture, which may hold negative energy from the past, and try to live without tables or shelves made from transparent plastic or glass: these symbolize lack of support and popularity. Heavy objects encourage permanence and stability, so a weighty piece of sculpture or even a large, smooth rock would earn its place.

Pictures, too, can influence a room: a mountain scene on the wall behind you represents support; hung in front of you, however, the same image denotes insurmountable barriers, so be careful. Like plants, a live aquarium symbolizes nature, and even a small one would be worth accommodating since water is a sign of money. To help create harmonious energy, play soothing background music while you work.

■ *Soft, pale ochre yellow is an excellent spiritual and aesthetic choice in a busy home office, where confidence and security are important considerations.*

119

■ *Try to keep the surface of your desk clear and the items you use most frequently close to hand. Here, a strategically placed bookshelf stores vital reference books neatly in the room's Knowledge corner.*

"WE MUST HAVE ORDER, ALLOCATING TO EACH THING ITS PROPER PLACE AND GIVING TO EACH THING ITS DUE ACCORDING TO ITS NATURE."

LUDWIG MIES VAN DER ROHE

THE HARMONIOUS DESK

Use the general principles of feng shui, scaled down and adapted, to select and organize your work surface. Try to find a desk made of solid wood (hardwood if possible), which symbolizes healthy growth. If your field is artistic, consider a round desk, which will encourage creativity; round tables are also excellent for meetings, since they foster harmony and strong teamwork. If your business is very exacting or involves a lot of figure work, the conventional rectangular or square surface is a wiser choice.

A cluttered desk, like an untidy room, will engender confusion and misunderstanding. For maximum benefit, keep the surface immediately in front of you completely clear of extraneous material, and position the things around you according to the bagua chart (see page 114). Keep things like invoices, chequebooks, quotations and contracts in the Wealth area in the top left-hand corner. Put the telephone at your immediate right (in the Helpful People corner) or place a lucky crystal here to enhance your professional relationships; keep any reference material that you use regularly – a dictionary or stocklist perhaps – in the Knowledge corner.

When your desk faces an inauspicious feature, such as a projecting corner or a column, try positioning a plant or a small bunch of flowers to block the negative energy flowing in your direction. Placing a flowering plant on your desk just before the beginning of a new year will enhance your professional fortunes and bolster your career prospects significantly in the coming months.

■ *To help neutralize the negative effect of facing a wall, hang in front of you a peaceful bucolic landscape, ideally with a small river or stream running through it.*

Colour and pattern

Timid souls who are frightened of colour on the walls of the living room or the kitchen are even more likely to fall back on a white or an off-white scheme when it comes to their work space. While it would be wise to avoid overpowering any room you'll be occupying for long hours with dazzling hues that hurt your eyes and distract your attention, there's certainly no need to shy away from colour altogether. In fact, ending up with a neutral palette as an act of cowardice rather than a positive style choice is a sad waste of the most powerful decorating tool at your disposal.

■ *Most people are inspired by bright, fresh greens and blues; use them as supporting players in a light neutral scheme (above) or be more adventurous and give them the starring role (opposite).*

PLAYING TRICKS

Remember that colour is magic: it can work miracles on both the look of a room and the mood of its occupants. On a purely visual level, design wisdom holds that pale shades expand the apparent size of a room and deeper ones decrease it. While this is certainly true, it is not necessarily of overwhelming importance, nor does it always represent the most creative use of colour. Many a work space, for example, is tucked into a dim corner – under the stairs, perhaps, or in an attic or a basement. When you want to bring a small, dark space to life, a warm hue like clotted cream, banana yellow, soft peach or flesh pink is a more effective choice than white or beige, which tend to look grey in all but the most golden and abundant natural light. It's a rare room that gets too much sun, but if you work somewhere like a converted conservatory, cool it down with watery blue or subtle grey-green. In ordinary rooms, however, shades like this have a tendency to look rather cold, so opt for similar but warmer ones like soft aqua, tender leaf green or pale lilac.

To pull all the elements together and minimize visual clutter, use the same colour on the walls and the ceiling. This trick is effective for disguising uneven shapes and awkward architectural features like sloping ceilings and protruding corners. In the same way, give wall-fixed shelves a sleek built-in look and blend them into your scheme by painting them to match the walls.

CALM WORKING SPACES

■ *Pink richly deserves a chance to show
what it can do in rooms other than
bedrooms or bathrooms. While this large,
modern interior can carry off the dramatic
shades of cerise, there are many softer
tones of cameo, plaster and shell pink that
would suit a less imposing work space.*

124

■ *In a scheme that was inspired by the adjoining garden, soft green walls evoke freshness and harmony; silvery florists' buckets continue the theme (above). All-over colour treatments create visual order and increase the impression of space, and in this bedroom office the same blue has been used on the walls, the work surface and the cantilevered shelves (above right).*

The smaller your room and the more demands you make on its visual space, the more you will gain by keeping all the main colours close in tone. So, for example, choosing a subtle ochre for ceiling, walls and fitted storage, then adding a natural-coloured floor covering (waxed boards or flat-pile carpet) and furniture in pale wootl, will create a more harmonious effect than, say, a white ceiling with yellow walls, timber shelves, black furniture and a patterned rug. Like kitchens and bathrooms, work spaces invariably contain so many disparate bits and pieces that an unbroken sweep of background colour is usually the wisest choice.

COLOUR HARMONY

Individual colours can have powerful associations for most people. Sometimes these reactions are purely cultural or historical, (red for anger, white for purity, pink for femininity). At other times our responses are more personal and we are drawn to colours that conjure up happy memories or to those that flatter our complexion. But the study of colour psychology – the way people's emotions are affected by the hues that surround them – is slightly more complex. When it comes to interior decoration, green is the most likely colour to inspire feelings of calm and well-being; for this reason, it is the traditional choice for

■ *The horticulturist who created this study has used colour to link the space with the garden outside: the natural tones of oak, wicker and sisal, white architectural detailing that echoes the miniature fence and gate on the desk, and a stunning skyscape trompe l'oeil on the ceiling.*

■ *The shelves and work surface in this contemporary home office have been painted different fruity shades like lime, orange, grape, strawberry or melon to create an eye-catching pattern of stripes.*

the room in a theatre where nervous performers await their turn – the Green Room. Green also invokes the freshness of nature and spring growth, and studies have revealed strong associations with cleanliness, which is why it is used so widely in the packaging of soap and detergent. If you are attracted to green as your dominant colour, choose a soft shade rather than harsh lime or day-glo mint.

With its suggestions of water and sky, blue also inspires an atmosphere of cool tranquillity. To prevent this coolness from becoming a forbidding chill, however, avoid greyish shades like Wedgwood or airforce blue, and balance a dominant blue with warm hues and the naturally golden tones of wood and wicker.

In the same way that one blue can be calming while another is cold, yellow – the colour of sunshine and spring flowers – can have widely varying effects, according to the shade you choose. A very bright or acid yellow in large doses, for example, is likely to irritate or disturb, while a pale buttery gold or a rich earthy ochre is cheerful, optimistic and stimulating. Yellow is temperamental, though, and only the very warmest shades (some experts claim only those with an ochre base) will keep their warmth consistently, so beware: any paint that looks lemony in the tin is likely to take on a greenish tinge as soon as the natural light dims.

Closely related to yellow is orange, which in its pure state is probably too garish to dominate a working space; one of its more muted tints – apricot or russet, perhaps – would be ideal. By the same token, while an expanse of bright red might be too claustrophobic in a home office, accents of this colour work well on a rug, chair or cushions. Red's most appealing qualities (it suggests opulence and high spirits and, like yellow, offers warmth and stimulation) also survive in more low-key shades such as soft rose and terracotta.

STAYING NEUTRAL

Used skilfully and with conviction, a broadly neutral palette of creams, whites, beiges, browns and ivories can make a subtle, sophisticated and extremely successful scheme. But choosing neutrals is not necessarily the easiest option: they do not all blend harmoniously just because they are

A pale, neutral colour scheme can be one of the best ways to ensure a cool, tranquil working environment. In this understated room, solid expanses of creamy white are relieved by the warmer tones of coir, wood and raffia at floor level. Supporting the desk, brushed steel legs add a touch of soft sheen.

■ *In the loft studio of a Dutch painter/ceramicist, plain walls provide a good background for the eye-catching colours and patterns found on the artworks, table and chairs. Note the sculptural quality given to the spiral stairs by their bold colour.*

neutral. This is because there are hundreds of different shades of white and cream – some tinged with blue, some with pink, some with yellow and so forth. Browns can be very greeny or very yellowy, and the term 'beige' can be applied to everything from pinky grey to pale brown. A haphazard jumble of all these hues produces surprisingly unappealing results, so you need to devote just as much – and sometimes more – care to the coordination of a neutral scheme as you would to a stronger or more varied one.

PLAYING WITH PATTERN

For the same reason that very vivid colours are distracting when you're trying to concentrate, an obtrusive pattern in any form (or an assortment of different patterns) is unlikely to work well in an office. What looks charming in a living room or bedroom (or even in a cosy letter-writing corner) can give an untidy and unprofessional look to a serious working space, so avoid chintzy florals and garish abstracts and limit your use of pattern to low-key examples such as small checks, subtle stripes and the understated geometry of textured weaves.

■ *The wooden-clad walls and floor of this home office provide large, but subtle, areas of pattern formed by the directional interplay of one grain with another.*

Indulging your senses

At the end of a stressful day, pamper yourself with a welcome task, a cool glass of wine and the sight and smell of your favourite blooms.

No matter how much satisfaction you get from the work you do, there are always times when small worries and minor annoyances threaten to become overpowering anxieties. To prevent tension from building up unchecked, take advantage of all the ways in which your senses can be soothed. When you're feeling frazzled, take a break in a comfortable chair to relax or think through a problem, light a scented candle, play some soothing music or focus on a favourite picture or family photograph, and turn your work space into a haven of calm.

In a peaceful work space under the eaves, softly draped curtains and opulent textiles furnish a marked textural contrast to the bare expanses of plaster and wood.

TEXTURE

The degree to which individuals are affected by texture – and the textures they are drawn to – varies enormously: some people find playing with a piece of jewellery or stroking a shiny pebble or a polished crystal hypnotically relaxing (this is the theory behind worry beads), while others take comfort from the yielding softness of a chenille chair cover or a velvety cushion.

Even if you are not drawn to the tactile quality of any particular surface or object, it may be that simply surrounding yourself with surfaces you find especially pleasing (natural ones like coarse wool, waxed timber and knobbly wicker, or smooth, sleek ones like satiny stainless steel and glossy laminate) can help to control your stress and restore your equilibrium.

SCENT

Over the last few years, the widespread appreciation of aromatherapy as an effective complementary treatment has heightened awareness of the powerful and therapeutic effect that fragrance can have on both physical and mental well-being.

To sweeten the air around you, bring a hint of nature to your work space and encourage feelings of well-being, arrange scented plants or containers of lavender, rose petals or potpourri among your books and files. When you are feeling especially tense, sad or weary, permeate the atmosphere with an appropriate natural essence (see box below) by lighting a scented candle, warming a concentrated oil in a special burner, vaporizer or light-bulb ring, or adding a few drops of the oil to a bowl of water placed near a radiator or heating duct. (If you happen to have a humidifier in the room, add a little perfumed oil to the water when you refill it.)

Those who depend on the constant inhalation of nicotine to get them through the working day might try to counteract some of its negative effects by installing a small air purifier.

HEALING VAPOURS

For centuries, natural plant essences in the form of essential oils have been used to promote relaxation and well-being. These highly distilled oils are very concentrated, and, as a general rule, they should not be taken internally or applied directly to your skin. To help you function more efficiently, experiment with the following plants:

CLARY SAGE	*A powerful treatment for anxiety and muscular tension*
DILL	*Both calming and refreshing*
JASMINE	*A remedy for anxiety linked to depression*
LAVENDER	*One of the best-known natural relaxants, it is also one of the few oils that can be used neat on your skin. Keep a bottle handy to rub on your wrists and temples as soon as you feel the panic start to rise*
LEMON & LIME	*Both are tangy, refreshing and ideal for mornings when you can't seem to galvanize your energies*
ROSE	*For worry, stress and low spirits*
ROSEMARY	*An invigorating oil that is also excellent for headaches and depression*
THYME	*To strengthen and stimulate*

Other useful relaxing oils are aniseed, fennel, frankincense, mandarin, melissa (lemon balm) and rosewood; for stimulation, you could also try bergamot, black pepper, chamomile and nutmeg.

On warm summer afternoons, the
French windows to this pretty brick-paved
terrace are opened wide so that the scents
of the garden can drift into the study.

"SILENCE MORE MUSICAL THAN
ANY SONG."

CHRISTINA ROSSETTI

■ *When tension mounts and concentration
starts to fade, the amateur musician
who works here stops to enjoy a short
musical interlude.*

SOUND

Sound can play one of two contrasting roles in your working life. When it takes the form of intrusive noise invading your sanctuary from elsewhere, it can be intensely irritating. As part of a considered and controlled sensory environment, however, sound may help you to feel more peaceful and productive.

Unfortunately, sound is more easily kept in than out, so it is much more effective to insulate a space where noise originates than one where noise is unwelcome. If possible, therefore, muffle a blaring television or radio by fixing a lining of some kind (purpose-made insulation, maybe, or timber cladding) to the walls of the relevant room. If this is not practical (or if the offending sounds are coming from outside your home), lining your own work space in this way will certainly help. A solid wall of books, as well as making good use of space, provides effective insulation, especially if the shelves are backed with a layer of cork or thick padding. More noise seeps in from around a room's entrance than through the walls, however; if it is causing you serious disturbance, consider investing in special double-door soundproofing.

If your principal distraction is the general clatter of family life, making sure that all the floors are fitted with thick carpet and underlay, particularly in heavy traffic areas like hallways and stairs, will make an appreciable difference. Curtains – at a window or a door – will also help to absorb unwanted noise.

Some people find a low level of carefully chosen background music enormously soothing while they work. If your only comparable experience involved the unwelcome infliction of other people's musical tastes in an open-plan office, it might be worth experimenting with a few of your own CDs, or searching out a radio station with a sympathetic playlist. Even if you need total silence for the more challenging aspects of your job, you may enjoy being in touch with the outside world occasionally through the radio, or find yourself inspired by a burst of your favourite composer when your spirits are flagging or the tasks at hand are boring and repetitious.

You should give serious consideration to ways in which you can reduce distracting background noise. Cork tiles are ideal for muffling unwanted sound. Try covering a floor-to-ceiling expanse with them to make a giant pinboard (left), or use them behind a solid wall of books to reinforce the insulation these shelves provide (below).

Camouflage and concealment

■ *A simple screen will afford a measure of privacy to a compact working corner and conceal it from view when relaxation is the order of the day (left).*

■ *Being able to close the door on bulky office equipment can be aesthetically and psychologically rewarding, especially if you are operating in a small space. Crafted in walnut, this elegant work-station cabinet represents a perfect fusion of oriental proportion and detailing with the pared-down efficiency of classic modern furniture (below).*

Most people who work at home, particularly those who don't have the advantage of a separate room, want at some time to conceal the resulting, often untidy, physical evidence. And even if you're happy to accept the aesthetics of office equipment and accessories within a domestic environment, you would be wise to conceal any expensive equipment behind a high screen or bookcase so that it can't be seen through the window by any would-be burglars. This is especially important if your work space is situated in a ground-floor room overlooking either the street or a secluded side or back area.

SUCCESSFUL SCREENING

One of the most effective ways to minimize the visual impact of a work area is to contain all of it – desk, equipment and storage capacity – inside a purpose-designed cabinet with doors that close neatly on the lot. These specialist units, which resemble a large wardrobe or armoire, are widely available in a variety of traditional and contemporary styles. If you want (and you can afford) a design that fulfils your needs and suits your style requirements exactly, it might be worth commissioning a custom-made piece from a furniture designer or craftsperson.

These self-contained units, no matter how capacious, are really only suitable for small-scale operations, however; full-sized work spaces are not so easy to hide away. If your work area is situated at one end of a large room, or in a deep alcove (like the short arm of an L-shape), explore ways of dividing the space off. The most elaborate arrangement is full-height folding or sliding doors that pull shut when necessary (if there is no window at the end where you work, be sure to allow for some kind of ventilation). Just as effective visually, and considerably easier and less costly to install, are long curtains, hung from a ceiling-fixed track. Alternatively, if the room is narrow enough, a high, wide screen would serve the same purpose.

Solutions like this are less appealing, however, when you want to maintain the impression of open space in a multi-purpose area such as a living room. But you can still use cleverly positioned items of furniture to screen the worst of the chaos – and often define different areas of use at the same time. Even a high-backed sofa, for example, will afford some discreet camouflage, while a free-standing set of shelves would fulfil both these functions and provide extra storage capacity as well. Choose a completely open unit that affords access from both sides, or one with a solid back that can double up as a useful office bulletin board.

■ *On this Portuguese rococo escritoire, the hinged flap provides a generous writing surface. When it's not in use, this section folds up to conceal clutter and link the top and bottom of the piece with a decorative angled panel (above).*

■ *Hinged floor-to-ceiling panels can be pulled closed to form a giant screen or left open, as here, to define the work and living areas without closing them off completely.*

Another particularly flexible and capacious option is a cube storage system, which works equally well in top-of-the-range timber or funky plastic. Stack the units up to chest or shoulder height, and arrange access from both sides by positioning them to face alternate directions. Available ready made or custom built, these modular units often feature different-sized compartments and have the additional advantage of considerable depth, so the top surface can accommodate bulky items like a printer or fax machine as well as filing trays and box files. When your work load

■ *A tiny working corner is set off from the main living area by a freestanding shelf unit on castors. The stylish magnetic pinboard has been cut from a sheet of roofing zinc.*

■ *Assembled from the same range of cube storage units that forms the adjacent library shelves, this stepped divider conceals an additional work surface and filing area from public view.*

and your budget expand, it's very easy to add more units (making sure you never pile them so high that they become unstable). Then, when you want to rearrange your space or move to another one, you can dismantle and reassemble the cubes. On a more modest level, consider disguising a wall of hard-working, probably messy, shelves by installing a roller blind or a simple curtain that can be pulled into position to cover them instantly.

When it comes to giving an impression of general untidiness and disorder in your work space, it's difficult to beat a pile of work in progress and a collection of writing implements and stationery supplies spread out on your

work surface. Instead of clearing everything away at the end of the working day to make a living room or bedroom look presentable, simply cover your desk with a large square of fabric chosen to coordinate with the room's other soft furnishings. This could be a hemmed length of one of the materials used elsewhere in the room, or a ready-made item such as a small tablecloth or even a big scarf or shawl. If your work station is situated in a separate room that doubles as guest accommodation, these instant camouflage techniques can save you from having to down tools for a major tidy-up every time visitors come to stay.

Ceiling-fixed curtains offer maximum flexibility since they can effectively screen off a working corner, yet are quick and easy to draw aside when you want to use the whole room.

Storage with style

When you're planning any kind of office, storage is one of the most vital elements, and a large proportion of the furnishings and equipment you acquire will fulfil some kind of storage function, from cabinets and shelf units to drawers, cupboards, boxes, racks, files and trays. In institutional work places, storage facilities usually tend to be functional but uninspiring, the design circumscribed for reasons of practicality or cost, or for the sake of corporate uniformity. But when you work at home, even though your storage requirements are just as exacting, you can make more creative and interesting design choices that will give your work space an identity all of its own.

KEEPING RECORDS STRAIGHT

When it comes to a home for your hanging files, there's no need to settle for a grey metal box – many office furnishers carry an impressive selection of funky colours as well. Or choose wooden filing drawers instead; modern, mass-produced versions are not much more expensive, although handsome old-fashioned models trimmed with brass, which are ideal for a domestic setting, are costly and becoming increasingly hard to find. If your budget is stretched, rescue a tired metal cabinet (two or four drawer) from a second-hand office furnisher and give it a new finish with car spray paint. This is very

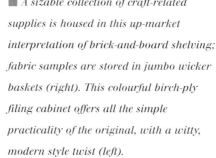
■ *A sizable collection of craft-related supplies is housed in this up-market interpretation of brick-and-board shelving; fabric samples are stored in jumbo wicker baskets (right). This colourful birch-ply filing cabinet offers all the simple practicality of the original, with a witty, modern style twist (left).*

easy to use and is available in a vast range of exciting colours from rich dark green and maroon to fresh zingy limes and oranges, sugar-almond pastels and classy neutrals like cream, taupe and glossy black.

Alternatively, look for ingenious hanging files concealed inside a rattan chest, a wooden blanket box or an upholstered ottoman. Remember that, even without a hanging frame, capacious chests and boxes like these are incredibly useful for storing old files or stationery supplies – and they provide an extra surface or seat at the same time.

SHELF ROOM

If it's freestanding shelves you need, consider those intended for use in warehouses and factories. These have a rough charm, a rugged practicality and an infinite flexibility in use that is almost impossible to find in ranges intended for domestic or office use. One of the most popular industrial

CALM WORKING SPACES

■ *Clear the decks by storing all your
small stationery supplies in a desk-top
drawer unit; old ones like this were often
designed to hold tiny craft or machine
components (left).*

■ *Keep an eye on your store cupboard for
smart tins that you can recycle as pen pots;
to keep them out of the way, attach them to
a stainless-steel magnetic board (below).*

shelving systems comes in the form of components of various heights, depths
and widths; you bolt them together like the pieces of a giant building set to
achieve the size and shape of unit you need.

Among the most useful items commonly sold by architectural salvage
dealers (or in second-hand furniture shops) are storage units that have been
removed from old shops, schools or public buildings like libraries. These
fittings, which are often made from solid wood, range from plain sets of
shelves and cupboards to glass-fronted display cases and rows of drawers
and cubby-holes of various sizes.

BE CREATIVE

In many cases, you can fulfil your storage needs and create a fresh, stylish
look at the same time by improvising and adapting items intended for use
elsewhere. Instead of shop-bought filing trays, for example, take advantage of
the spare, no-nonsense design of aluminium cake tins or baking dishes; for a
warmer look, choose shallow wicker trays intended for use in the garden, or
plywood fruit crates adorned with jolly labels. Keep urgent bills and letters
under your nose in a toast rack made from decorative earthenware or mirror-
finish chrome, and stick your pens and pencils in a pretty jug, a terracotta

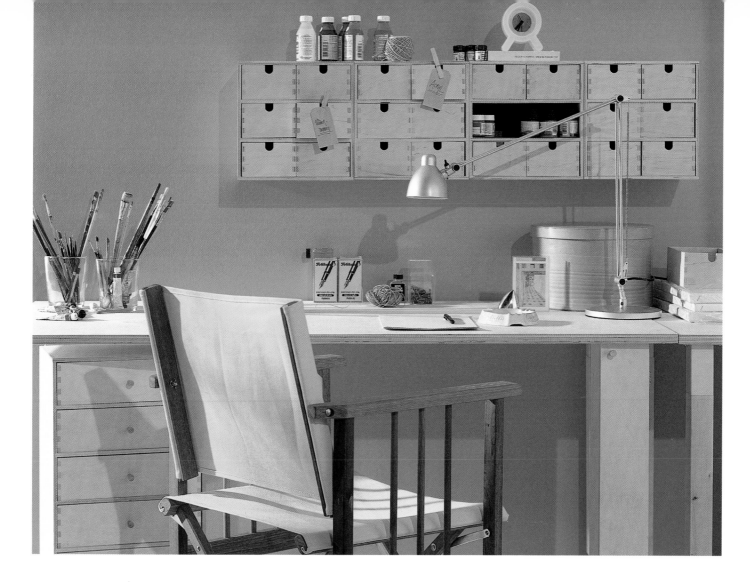

flower pot, a French café glass or an empty tin can with an appealing design. To swallow up waste paper, try a big bucket or pail made from cool galvanized metal or cheerful plastic; if you need a larger capacity, use an industrially inspired design intended for the kitchen, a traditional metal or plastic rubbish bin, or a small log basket.

A set of mini plywood drawers keeps an artist's supplies organized and close at hand. Units like this can be left in their pale, unfinished state or customized with paint, stain, oil or wax.

CHOOSE YOUR MOOD

Before the explosion of interest in the home-office market, the range of storage accessories available was severely limited. Recently, though, it seems as if every fashionable store and catalogue is offering a range of coordinating boxes, wallets, files, notebooks and binders. Whether your taste runs to understated textures, plain colours, country-garden flowers or exotic animal prints, there is certain to be something on the market for you. In most cases, one or two of these items is enough to brighten a dull desk or add a touch of glamour to the filing, but if you decide to go for a complete collection of matching accessories, it might be a good idea to stockpile extra supplies when you make your initial purchases; fashion-inspired lines like these usually have a very short span of availability, so you may not be able to extend your storage capacity in the future or replace individual items.

"A PLACE FOR EVERYTHING AND EVERYTHING IN ITS PLACE."
MRS BEETON

Use your imagination to find ingenious storage solutions that fulfil their practical function and complement the style you've chosen for your work space. You may *discover that some of the most ingenious ideas – like using painted garden trellis as a pinboard – are also the most eye-catching and affordable.*

The personal touch

■ *Surrounding yourself with things you love is bound to enhance your productivity and galvanize your creative energy. Here, extravagant Baroque curves (opposite) and the more refined shapes associated with classical antiquity (left) provide their owners with visual inspiration.*

One of the obvious advantages of setting up a work space at home is that you can give it a far stronger sense of your own personality than would ever be appropriate in a corporate environment. Home workers who regularly see clients on the premises are likely to require more strictly professional sur-roundings than those who beaver away in solitude, but as long as you don't introduce unnecessary distractions, or compromise on safety or practicality, there's no reason why you can't interpret a wide range of office furnishing conventions in your own highly original way. Splash out on an unusual telephone or calculator, for example, or a quirky mouse mat in the form of a

"IT IS IMPOSSIBLE TO ENJOY
IDLING THOROUGHLY UNLESS
ONE HAS PLENTY OF WORK
TO DO."

JEROME K. JEROME

■ *Featuring a cheerful gingham-covered
pinboard, this peaceful and personal
corner of a child's room provides plenty
of scope for creative work and play.*

favourite cartoon character or painting. If you have suitable software (or
know someone who does), create your own screensaver from a family
photograph, a child's drawing or any other image that gives you pleasure.

As with any room, one of the most effective ways to add warmth and individuality to your work area is with textiles. An exotic rug, for instance, can
transform a small space, and many cotton ones are so inexpensive that you
can replace them when they get grubby or worn out, or you just fancy a
change. Many firms who supply office chairs are willing to cover them in your
own choice of fabric, so you can reject the tweedy samples on offer in favour

■ *A simple but dramatic display of vivid blooms in richly hued glass vases stamp this correspondence desk with the owner's distinctive style.*

CALM WORKING SPACES

■ *An exotic blend of bamboo and cane with dark wood furniture and oriental pottery gives a distinctive colonial look to this spacious and comfortable home office. Note the small woven chest that conceals a useful hanging file system.*

of a jewel-hued cotton velvet, a slinky zebra stripe or an extravagant floral print. (Or, if your existing chair has a simple, separate seat and back, make your own covers that slip into place like big shower caps.) Create a dramatic pinboard by stapling a length of material over a large piece of cork or softboard. If you can sew, make bespoke dust covers for your computer equipment, using the boring plastic ones as templates, or simply replace the existing covers with squares of colourful fabric.

To encourage the calming effect of nature and soften the hard-edged look that too much modern technology can produce, display a collection of low-maintenance house plants. (Not only will they give you something to

focus on when your spirits are flagging, they'll also help to replace some of the moisture that electrical equipment in constant use removes from the atmosphere.) If surface space is in short supply, go for large specimens in floor-standing tubs, or fix deep, sturdy shelves at picture-rail height and fill them with shade-loving plants that trail over the edges; to avoid adding to your work load unnecessarily, be sure to choose containers that are big enough not to require daily watering. Fresh flowers will provide a delightful burst of colour and fragrance, but be careful to keep them away from anything electrical – an accidental spill could cause a short in your power supply and disable your equipment.

The cutting room

Clever planning and neat, multi-purpose furnishings make it possible for this small room to include flexible work areas that can be easily tucked away when not in use. To create a square surface for sewing or paperwork, two narrow wheeled tables clip together. When a smaller work station is required, one of them slots into a slim cabinet at the end of a bed to form a desk.

When neither table is in use, they slide into a gap in the specially designed wall-fixed storage unit, which also accommodates a useful hanging rack.

■ *Fixed to the wall, an adjustable lamp provides illumination for bedtime reading and swivels slightly to serve as a task light for the adjoining work surface (above). The sewing machine tucks neatly into the cupboard underneath when it's not needed.*

■ *A row of bull-dog clips holds treasured pictures and cards and keeps small, easily lost items out of harm's way (left).*

■ *Chosen to integrate with the room's overall colour and design, the cupboards are in fact units from an inexpensive kitchen range and provide maximum storage capacity in a limited space (opposite).*

Work-space
basics

BEFORE YOU BEGIN to put into practice all your careful organization, product research and design flair, there are a number of practical issues that every home worker should consider. Safety and security are of paramount importance, as is ensuring that your home office is a comfortable temperature. This section will also help you to familiarize yourself with the guidelines covering such things as access and clearance, tax and insurance; depending on the size and nature of your business, your office area may even be subject to regulations of some kind set down by your local planning authority.

Floor planning

■ *This executive work space was planned to include plenty of storage and filing units near the desk for convenient access. The designer responsible also made sure that each drawer and door could be opened freely without getting in the way or posing a safety hazard.*

I n order to establish a feasible floor plan for your working space, you will need to measure every piece of furniture that has to be accommodated. Mark on your plan where such things as power points and light fittings and switches are situated, and indicate the position of doors, windows and wall-fixed items like shelves and cupboards.

Before you arrive at your final arrangement, however, you should also take into account the amount of room each article will require for safe and convenient circulation, access and, where relevant, clearance. Ignoring these guidelines, however strong the temptation, will increase significantly your risk of minor mishaps such as bruising your knee when you swivel in your chair or banging your head when you stand up suddenly. Accidents like these, when they occur rarely, cause no more than minor annoyance; when they happen all the time, they amount to grounds for a complete rethink of the room's layout.

GROUND RULES

■ Allow at least 1m (39in) between your task chair and a wall or another piece of furniture so that you can get in and out and lean back easily.

■ To ensure a safe passage between two pieces of furniture or a piece of furniture and a wall, allow a corridor of at least 60cm (24in).

■ Allow at least 1m (39in) in front of a filing cabinet so that you can use the drawers comfortably.

■ Allow at least 90cm (36in) in front of a set of shelves for easy access.

■ An internal door usually opens into a room, so remember to allow for clearance equal to about twice its width.

■ If you sit directly facing a wall, you won't be able to reach anything that is pinned or hung on it if your desk is more than about 75cm (30in) deep.

■ Each person seated at a meeting table needs about 75cm (30in) to manoeuvre comfortably.

163

Safety

■ *If you need regular access to high-level storage, never rely on piles of books or a wobbly chair to stand on. Invest in a purpose-designed ladder or a pair of library steps (below).*

At every stage of your office planning and furnishing, it's vital that you bear in mind the relevant safety considerations.

Before you set up shop, make sure you have plenty of power points, and check that they are in the right places: overloaded sockets and long extension leads are both highly dangerous. In any case, the last thing you want is to add to the spaghetti of wires and flexes that is required to supply modern communications and information technology, as well as ordinary domestic items such as lamps, kettles and sound systems.

Many purpose-built computer desks and work stations have an integral channelling system to contain and protect these cables. If you don't use one of these, you can buy channelling separately, or try winding the wires around a cable roller (which looks like a big plastic yo-yo); alternatively, improvise by running them through a length of plastic pipe or ducting, or anchoring them along the skirting board under a simple cover that lifts up to allow access. Whatever solution you choose, it's important to avoid scrunching cables into a small or

■ *Guard against electrical fires, protect your equipment and avoid irritating and potentially hazardous tangles of wires and cables by choosing a work station that features a cable port (left and far left). Some route the cables vertically through the leg frame (below).*

enclosed space, since this makes them particularly vulnerable to damage and over-heating. Similarly, never get rid of unsightly flexes by running them under a rug or carpet. Not only does this create friction on the wiring, which is a serious fire hazard, it also leaves a bumpy, uneven surface that at worst can trip you up and at best will leave you with worn strips across the carpet pile. Remember, too, that any rug placed on a hard floor should have an anti-slip mat underneath. These are available in a number of stock sizes and often cut to length as well.

Ventilation is another important consideration. Make sure plenty of cool air can circulate around anything electrical, again to guard against over-heating. (For the same reason, try to keep electrical equipment out of direct sunlight and away from direct heat sources.) Ventilation is particularly necessary in work spaces that feature things like laser printers and photocopiers, which, as well as creating heat, pollute the air by emitting ozone.

In any room that contains a number of electrical appliances, it is worth investing in a smoke alarm. Lightweight and easy to install, these should ideally be fixed to the ceiling or high up on a wall.

If you're operating in a restricted space, try to avoid furniture and fittings with sharp corners, especially at head- and eye-level. Any existing corners that habitually attack you can be disarmed with special safety covers intended to protect small children. Don't overcrowd surfaces, especially those above shoulder height, and never create teetering towers of books and files that could collapse onto a piece of expensive equipment – or your head.

Heating and cooling

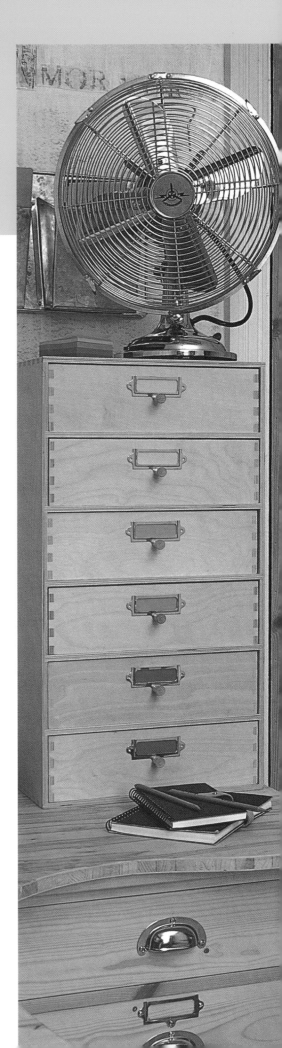

Temperature control is of paramount importance in a working environment. Certainly, no matter how skilfully you design and furnish your work area, you'll never feel comfortable and relaxed there – or be able to work productively – if it is unbearably chilly in winter or oppressively hot during the summer months. And even if you suffer only in extreme weather, it's well worth tackling the problem rather than stoically pulling on an extra sweater or constantly fanning yourself with the filing.

Begin by checking the condition of all windows and doors: if there are gaps around either, howling draughts will get through. (At the same time, make sure that your windows open freely to admit fresh air and cooling breezes when necessary.) Many draught-busting tactics are comparatively simple, such as fixing insulating strips around each window and hanging long, thick curtains (both of which are effective for draughty internal doors as well). Ground-level gales can be blocked with some form of draught excluder placed against the bottom of the door – in emergencies, a rolled-up towel will do. At the other end of the scale, you might decide to replace any ill-fitting doors or windows completely, or install double-glazing, which also cuts out a considerable amount of noise.

If the room you work in is never really warm enough, think about adding another radiator or replacing the existing one with a larger, more efficient model. You could also invest in a portable heater that lives there permanently; then, when the temperature drops, you won't have to waste time trying to locate it or arguing with other household members about whose need for it is more pressing.

■ *To provide plenty of warmth and a sculptural addition to your scheme, look for a linear radiator you can mount on the wall (far left), or a portable heater with funky retro styling (left).*

It is equally difficult to concentrate on your work in the stifling heat, so if you know you're going to suffer when the temperature soars, it is worth installing some sort of cooling system. An electric fan (floor-standing, table-top or mounted on the wall or ceiling) will bring some degree of relief. If you live in a particularly warm climate – or if you are especially sensitive to the heat – it may be worth investing in a proper air-conditioning system. Choose from a fixed model that fits inside an existing window, or a mobile unit that can be moved around the room and used elsewhere in your home as well. Shutters and blinds will also help to block out the intensity of the sun's rays.

■ *In a work space that shares its quarters with the kitchen, a handsome solid fuel-burning stove provides valuable warmth in the colder months (right).*

Security

■ *If you regularly store confidential files or items of value, make sure there is at least one secure drawer or cupboard where they can be locked away (left).*

U nder any circumstances, having your home broken into is a major shock, and the loss, inconvenience and stress that result can affect your life for a considerable period. The consequences of losing not only money, valuables and personal documents but all your business equipment, your current work and your records as well are much more serious. Even if you can replace things like a computer or printer as soon as possible, your business is bound to be interrupted. No matter how stretched you are for money or time, therefore, be sure to make adequate provision for security. The peace of mind that comes from knowing your property is adequately protected will more than repay the investment.

Clearly, when both your home and your livelihood are involved, it is wise to invest in a comprehensive security system. Free advice about which ones will best suit your needs, and a list of reputable security firms in your area, are usually available from your local police or your insurance company. If you approach any organization that does not come with this kind of recommendation, make sure it is a member of the relevant trade association.

Whatever the nature of the system you decide on (alarm, grilles, panic buttons, etc.) you should add locks to all your windows, even the smallest fanlights, since most burglars gain access this way. Always keep skylights and windows that are accessible from the ground or from an adjoining roof locked whenever the room is empty.

Fit front and back doors with strong deadlocks, plus bolts top and bottom and a security chain (or even an entryphone) so that you can confirm the identity of all strangers before you let them in. Check the

■ *If your work space is visible from the street, avoid keeping your expensive equipment on permanent display. A unit with sliding drawers allows valuables to be kept out of sight (left).*

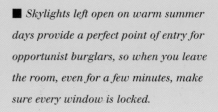

■ *Skylights left open on warm summer days provide a perfect point of entry for opportunist burglars, so when you leave the room, even for a few minutes, make sure every window is locked.*

Any item whose loss would create major problems should be kept in a safe or a lockable fireproof cabinet. This includes not only obvious things like cash, credit cards and cheques, but also photographic transparencies, one-off samples and disks containing important records, confidential information or irreplaceable work. Use a special security marker to label your valuables with your telephone number or your postcode, and take colour photographs of any unusual items so that they are easier to identify if they are found.

Every time you go away, cancel all your deliveries; also invest in a time switch to turn your lights on and off. You could also ask the police to put your house on its unattended premises register – with luck, they may be willing to drive past often enough to discourage any potential thieves keeping watch.

strength of the door hinges as well, and make sure that they are well secured – the most sophisticated locks are useless if the door can be kicked in easily. Remember that patio doors are especially vulnerable, so they should be fitted with special patio-door locks top and bottom.

It's also a good idea to fit secure locks on the internal door of the room where you keep your computer equipment; that way, even if burglars get in through a window, they will have to struggle to lift heavy, bulky machines out the same way.

Never leave a garage or garden shed unsecured, since ladders and spades are ideal burglars' tools, and fit security lights to the front, back and sides of the building to prevent intruders from working under cover of darkness.

Finance and law

When it comes to dealing with officialdom, begin by examining any paperwork that deals with the occupancy of your home, such as a tenancy agreement, a lease, a deed or a mortgage. In theory, any of these documents could contain a clause that prevents you from using the premises for commercial activity, but it's much more likely that you will simply be required to let your landlord or mortgage lender know what you intend to do.

If you are looking to buy somewhere to convert for genuine mixed use – a home with a shop attached, perhaps – you may find it more difficult to arrange a mortgage in the first place. There should be no problems, though, if all you have in mind is a single-person operation in a spare room.

INSURANCE

Look carefully at your house insurance: most policies do not include work-related cover and some expressly exclude computer equipment. If you're very unlucky, your policy might even state that working from home invalidates your normal cover. (On the plus side, some companies are prepared to negotiate a reduction in your premiums if you've added an alarm system or other security measures, or on the grounds that the premises are regularly occupied during the day.) Establish with your insurer whether you can alter your existing policy to accommodate a new home-working arrangement, or if you need to make separate insurance arrangements, perhaps by taking out a purpose-designed policy. At the same time, check to see if you should arrange special cover for anything you regularly remove from your base, like a laptop computer or a mobile phone.

In addition to contents insurance, think about arranging cover for employee liability if you intend to employ casual help during busy

LOCAL PLANNING OR ZONING

On the whole, planning approval is not necessary for home workers. Most local or municipal authorities, however, have a different set of rules and regulations for domestic and commercial premises, and there are some circumstances under which they will not allow business activity in domestic buildings. As a rough guide, you are likely to be affected if:

- *your business takes up most of your home*
- *you employ other people*
- *you have a significant number of visitors*
- *your business involves collections and/or deliveries that cause parking or traffic problems*
- *your business creates persistent noise or disturbance that affects your neighbours*
- *you make significant alterations to your home or its site*
- *you display obtrusive signs or advertisements.*

If you have any doubts, talk over your plans with the relevant authorities. Often, when there are areas of concern, they can be dealt with by negotiation; you may have to limit visitors to certain hours, for example, or settle for a discreet sign instead of an eye-catching banner.

periods, or public liability if you expect to entertain clients or other visitors. Many prudent home workers also insure against loss of revenue if they are injured or fall ill, or as a result of a burglary or fire. Remember that damage to your accounts records alone could plunge you into cash-flow chaos.

TAX

While tax regulations vary, you can usually claim as legitimate expenses any equipment, furnishings, stationery and supplies directly connected with your work. This includes not only obvious things like your desk, your chair and your computer equipment, but also decorating expenses like paint, fabric, plants and pictures, and even the supplies you need to make tea and coffee, if they're used exclusively in your office.

A proportion of some household bills can usually be set off against tax as well, according to how much of your home is occupied by your business. So, if you work in one room of a five-room house, you might be able to claim 20 per cent of the cost of your heating and power. Similarly, if you have only one telephone line, establish how much of the bill is tax deductible by adding up the cost of the work-related calls and adding an appropriate proportion of the line rental.

When you come to sell your home, any area set aside solely for business could, in theory, attract some

kind of transfer or capital gains tax. You can often get around this, however, if the room also has some domestic function – a work space that occasionally doubles up as a guest room, for instance.

Stockists

GENERAL

AEROMAIL
46 Weir Road
Wimbledon
London SW19 8UG
Tel: 020 8971 0066
Fax: 020 8971 0044
www.aero-furniture.com
*Furniture and desk
assessories; mail order*

ALMO OFFICE
168 Drury Lane
London WC2B 5OA
Tel: 020 7831 6200
Fax: 020 7430 2199
Almooffice.cablenet.co.uk
*General office supplies;
mail order*

ATRIUM
Centrepoint
22–24 St Giles High St
London WC2H 8LN
Tel: 020 7379 7288
www.atrivm.co.uk
Office chairs

BEDFORD AND SOAR
David Road
Poyle Trading Estate
Colnbrook
Slough SL3 ODB
Tel: 01753 680666
www.bedford.shelf.co.uk
Industrial shelving systems

BUREAU (AND BRANCHES)
10 Great Newport Street
London WC2H 7JA
Tel: 020 7836 3502
Fax: 020 7836 8765
*Stationery and office
furniture; mail order*

CENTA GRAPH
18 Station Parade
Harrogate HG1 1UE
Tel: 01423 566527
Fax: 01423 505486
*Specialist graphics
stationery*

**CHRISTOPHER WRAY
LIGHTING**
591–593 King's Road
London SW6 2YW
Tel: 020 7736 8434

Fax: 020 7731 3507
www.christopher-
wray.com

COEXISTENCE
288 Upper Street
London N1 2TZ
Tel: 020 7354 8817
Fax: 020 7354 9610
www.coexistence.co.uk
*Office furniture – by
appointment only*

THE CONRAN SHOP
Michelin House
Fulham Road
London SW3 6RD
Tel: 020 7589 7401
www.conran.co.uk
*Modern furniture and
office accessories*

**CUBESTORE STORAGE
SYSTEMS**
58 Pembroke Road

London W8
Tel: 020 7602 2001
www.cubestore.com
Modular storage systems

DIRECTIVE OFFICE
3 Rufus St.
London N1 6PE
Tel: 020 7613 2888
Fax: 020 7613 1506
*Electronic equipment
and furniture*

GEOFFREY DRAYTON
85 Hampstead Road
London NW1 2PL
Tel: 020 7387 5840
Fax: 020 7387 5874
*Modern classic office
furniture*

**HABITAT UK LTD (AND
BRANCHES)**
196 Tottenham Court Rd
London W1P 9LD
Tel: 020 7255 2545
www.habitat.net

HERMAN MILLER
149 Tottenham Court Rd

London W1P 0JA
Tel: 020 7388 7331
Fax: 020 7387 3507
www.millereurope.co.
uk/shop
*Modern classic office
furniture*

**THE HOLDING COMPANY
MAIL ORDER**
Burlington House
184 New Kings Road
London SW6 4NF
Tel: 020 7610 9160
Fax: 020 7610 9166
www.theholdingcompany.
co.uk
Storage; mail order

THE HOME OFFICE
TempleCo Ten Limited
Stonestile Barn
Harthill
Charing
Kent TN27 OHW
Tel: 01233 712710
Fax: 01233 712711
www.thehomeofficecomp
any.com
Modular buildings

**HOMELODGE BUILDINGS
LIMITED**
Kingswell Point
Crawley
Winchester
Hampshire SO21 2PU
Tel: 01962 881480
Fax: 01962 889070
Modular buildings

**HUBBARD'S OFFICE
FURNITURE**
187–199 Gray's Inn Road
London WC1 X8UL
Tel: 020 7837 4366
Fax: 020 7837 5994
*New and second-hand
furniture*

**IKEA BRENT PARK (AND
BRANCHES)**
2 Drury Way
North Circular Road
London NW10 0TN
www.ikea.com
Tel: 020 8208 5600
Fax: 020 233 2243
*Home-office furniture,
storage*

JOHN LEWIS
Oxford Street
London W1A 1EX
Tel: 020 7629 7711
Fax: 020 7514 5300
www.johnlewis.co.uk

JUST DESKS
20 Church St
London NW8 8EP
Tel: 020 7723 7976
Fax: 020 7402 646
*Traditional office
furniture*

**KCS – TOOLS FOR THE
COMPUTER-ENABLED**
Freepost
Southampton SO17 1YA
Tel: 023 8058 4314
Fax: 023 8058 4320
www.keytools.com
*Equipment to suit RSI
and special needs;
mail order*

LANGFORD & HILL
38-40 Warwick Street
London W1R 6JT
Tel: 020 7437 9945
Fax: 020 7734 5543
www.langfordhill.co.uk
Graphic supplies

LONDON GRAPHIC CENTRE
16–18 Shelton St
Covent Garden
London WC1 9JJ
Tel: 020 7240 0095
Fax: 020 7831 1544
www.londongraphics.
co.uk
Stationery

**MARGOLIS OFFICE
INTERIORS LTD**
341 Euston Road
London NW1 3AD
Tel: 020 7387 8217
Fax: 020 7388 0625
www.cityscan.co.uk/
margolis-office-furniture

**MARKS & SPENCER
DIRECT**
FREEPOST, PO Box 288
Warrington
Cheshire WA1 2BR
Tel: 0345 902 902
Fax: 0345 904 904
customer.services@marks
-and-spencer.co.uk
www.marks-and-
spencer.co.uk
Mail order

MCCORD
London Road
Preston PR11 1RP
Tel: 0870 908 7005
Fax: 0870 908 7050
www.mccord.uk.com
*Foldaway offices,
storage; mail order*

MORGAN RIVER
Dulwich Road
London SE24 OPB
Tel: 020 7274 7607
Fax: 020 7738 6262
Furniture

MUJI
Unit 5
6 Tottenham Court Road
London W1
Tel: 020 7323 2208
Stationery & storage

**NEVILLE JOHNSON
OFFICES LTD**
Broadoak Business Park
Ashburton Road West
Trafford Park
Manchester M17 1RW
Tel: 0161 873 8333
Fax: 0161 873 8335

www.nevillejohnson.
co.uk
*Individually designed
home offices*

NEXT DIRECTORY
0845 6000 7000
www.next.co.uk
(for shop enquiries tel:
08702 435435)
Mail order

OCEAN HOME SHOPPING
Freepost
LON811
Tel: 0870 848 4840
Fax: 0870 848 4849
Storage; mail order

PAPERCHASE
14 Bank House
St Mary's Gate
Manchester M11PX
Tel: 0161 839 1500
Fax: 0161 839 2361
*Stationery; desk
accessories & storage*

PURVES & PURVES
Unit 4,
Minerva Business
Centre,
58–60 Minerva Road
London NW10 6HJ
Tel: 0870 603 0205
Fax: 020 8961 3443

www.purves.co.uk
Furniture; mail order

RYMAN
(Branches nationwide)
Tel: 020 569 3000
www.ryman.co.uk
Stationery

SHARPS HOME OFFICE
For a list of showrooms
contact the head office:
Albany Park
Camberley
Surrey GU15 2PL
Tel: 0800 9178 178
www.sharps.co.uk

SPACE2
Freepost CL3341
PO Box 99
Sudbury
Suffolk CO1O 6BR
Tel: 0800 0 28 20 22
Fax: 01787 378 426
info@space2.com
www.space2.com
*Computer furniture; mail
order*

STEELCASE STRAFOR
Newlands Drive
Poyle
Berks SL3
Tel: 020 7874 0000
Custom-built furniture

TEMPO
For stores throughout
London, the south and
the midlands:
Tel: 0990 435363
www.tempo.co.uk
Computers & accessories

VIADUCT FURNITURE
1–10 Summer's Street
London EC1
Tel: 020 7278 8456
*Adaptable home-office
furniture*

VIKING DIRECT
PO Box 187
Leicester LE4 1ZZ
Tel: 0800 424444
Fax: 0800 622211
www.viking-direct.co.uk
Stationery; mail order

TRADE ASSOCIATIONS
HOME BUSINESS ALLIANCE
The Firs
High Street
March, Cambridgeshire
PE15 9LQ
Tel: 01945 463303
Fax: 01945 474555
www.hba.org.uk

**BRITISH SECURITY
INDUSTRY ASSOCIATION**
Security House

Barbourne Road
Worcester WR1 1RS
Tel: 01905 21464
Fax: 01905 613625
www.bsia.co.uk
*Will provide a list of
local members*

Salvo
Tel: 01890 820333
www.salvo.co.uk
*Lists nationwide salvage
yards*

COMPUTER AND
SOFTWARE
HELPLINES
APPLE MACINTOSH
Tel: 0990 127753
www.apple.com

BT
Tel: 0800 800050
www.bt.com/home

IBM
Tel: 01475 555055
www.pc.ibm.com

MICROSOFT
Tel: 0870 6010100
www.microsoft.com

CANON
Tel: 0870 5143723
www.canon.com

Index

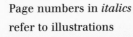

Acknowledgments

Picture credits:

The publisher would like to thank the following photographers and agencies for their kind permission to reproduce their pictures in this book.

a=above, b=below, l=left, c=centre, r=right

1 Ted Yarwood; 2-3 Paul Ryan/International Interiors (Designer: Jacqueline Morabito); 4al Camera Press; 4ac Camera Press; 6-7 Tim Beddow/Interior Archive; 8 Ted Yarwood (Design: Suzanne Dimma, Toronto); 9 Paul Ryan/International Interiors (Architects: Moneo & Brock); 10-11 Camera Press/Zuhause; 12 Camera Press/Brigitte; 13 Paul Ryan/International Interiors (Andre Balasz); 14 Camera Press/ Schöner Wohnen; 16 IPC Syndication/Homes & Gardens/Elizabeth Zeschin; 17 Ted Yarwood; 18-19 Sharps Home Office; 20 James Merrell/Narratives; 21 Camera Press; 22-23 Camera Press; 24 Tim Street-Porter (Nick Berman); 25 Paul Ryan/International Interiors (Designer: Maeve Mougin); 26 Camera Press; 27a Camera Press; 27b Camera Press; 28l Ted Yarwood (Design: Sarah Richardson, Toronto); 28r Tim Street-Porter (Nick Berman); 29 Ray Main/Mainstream (Iorino Design); 30-31 Corbis UK; 32 Paul Ryan/International Interiors (Elisa Corti); 33 Camera Press; 34 Edina van der Wyck/Interior Archive (Designer: Atlanta Bartlett); 35 Ted Yarwood; 36-37 Ted Yarwood (Design: Brian Brownlie, Toronto); 38l Camera Press/Living; 38r Camera Press; 39 Fritz von der Schulenburg/Interior Archive; 40 Camera Press; 41 Abode/Ian Parry; 42-43 'The Home Office' fromTempleCo Ten Limited; 44-45 Robert Harding Syndication/ Inspirations/Lizzie Orme; 46 Camera Press; 48a Paul Ryan/ International Interiors (Designer: Frances Halliday); 48b Marianne Majerus (Architect: Barbara Weiss); 49 View/Dennis Gilbert (Norman Foster Architects); 50 Camera Press; 51 Camera Press; 52 Paul Ryan/International Interiors (Abbi Zabar); 53 Camera Press; 54 Tom Leighton/John Lewis; 55 Ted Yarwood (Design: XTC Design, Toronto); 56al Verne/Houses & Interiors; 56bl Marianne Majerus; 56r Jan Baldwin/Narratives; 57 View/Chris Gascoigne (Simon Conder Associates); 58a Morgan River Ltd.; 58cl Margolis; 58cr Miller; 58b Morgan River Limited; 59 Camera Press/Suomen Kuvapalvelu; 60l Andrew Wood/Interior Archive (Owner: Brian Ma Siy); 60r Ted Yarwood; 61l IPC/Living Etc.; 61r Paul Ryan/International Interiors (Design: Victoria Hagan); 62a Margolis; 62b Simon Butcher/Houses & Interiors; 63 Simon Butcher/Houses & Interiors; 64-5 Camera Press; 66a Flos; Margolis; IPC Syndication; Margolis; 66b Verne/Houses & Interiors; 67 Cassina, Design: Philippe Starck (Ph: Tommaso Sarlori); 68-9 Paul Ryan/International Interiors (Designer: Gray Joop); 70al John Barker Anglepoise Ltd.; 70ac IPC Syndication/ Homes & Gardens; 70ar Flos; 70b IPC Syndication/Homes & Gardens; 71 Margolis; 72 IPC Syndication/Homes & Gardens/Jan Baldwin; 73 Christian Sarramon (Interior Designer: Christine Mengaud); 74bl Tim Street-Porter (Josh Schweitzer); 74-75 Steve Sparrow/Houses & Interiors; 76a Ted Yarwood; 76b Alan Weintraub/Arcaid; 77 Ted Yarwood; 78a Morgan River Ltd.; Purves & Purves (Design: Ron Arad); Past Times 01993 770440; Morgan River Ltd.; 78l Robert Harding Syndication/ Inspirations/Russell Sadur; 79 Alan Weintraub/Arcaid; 80 Morgan River Ltd.; 80b Past Times 01993 770440; 80-81 Camera Press/Fair Lady; 81r McCord by Mail; 82 Paul Ryan/International Interiors (Designer: Alex Vervoord); 83l IPC Syndication/Homes & Gardens/Simon Upton; 83r Ted Yarwood; 84l McCord by Mail; 84-85 Camera Press; 86 Margolis; 87 Space2.com; 88a Bruce Mackie; 88b Sharps Home Office; 89 Ted Yarwood; 90 Tom Leighton/John Lewis Department Stores; 92 Bruce Mackie; 93 Space2.com; 94 Lars Hallen; 95a McCord by Mail; 95b Margolis; 96-98al Margolis; 98ar Sharps Home Office; 98c Margolis; 98b Morgan River Ltd.; 99 Ted Yarwood; 100-101 John Lewis of Hungerford, Artisan Kitchens & Furniture; 102 Paul Ryan/International Interiors (Architect: Hariri & Hariri); 104 Deidi von Schaewen; 105 Camera Press/SHE; 106a View/Peter Cook; 106b Marianne Majerus (Architect: Alastair Howe); 107 IPC Syndication/Homes & Gardens/Andreas von Einsiedel; 108 Abode; 109 Paul Ryan/International Interiors (Designer: Sasha Waddell); 110-111 Roger Brooks/Houses & Interiors; 111r Simon Upton/Interior Archive (Owner: Annabel Astor); 112 Paul Ryan/International Interiors (Kristina & Bjorn Sahlquist); 113 Paul Ryan/International Interiors (Designer: Gus Baaker); 114-115 Christian Sarramon (Stylist: Brigitte Forgeur); 116-117 Camera Press/IMS; 119-120 Camera Press; 121 Verne/Houses & Interiors; 122 Camera Press/Journal Für Die Frau; 123 IPC Syndication/Homes & Gardens/Elizabeth Zeschin; 124-125 Verne/Houses & Interiors; 126l IPC Syndication/Homes & Gardens/James Merrell; 126r IPC Syndication/Living Etc./Neil Mersch; 127 Richard Felber; 128 IPC Syndication/Living Etc./Nick Pope; 129 Richard Davies; 130 Paul Ryan/International Interiors (Designer: Rob Brandt); 131 Richard Davies; 132-133 Camera Press; 134ar Robert Harding Picture Library; 134c Marshall Editions/Iain Pagnell; 134b Marshall Editions/Andrew Sydenham; 135-136 Richard Felber; 137a IPC Syndication/Homes & Gardens; 137b Michael Moran (Siegel Swansea Loft - Architects: Abelow Connors Sherman); 138l Andrew Wood/Interior Archive (Designer: Peter Wylly, Babylon Design); 138r and 139l Channels; 139r Corbis UK; 140 Abode; 141 Camera Press; 142 Richard Davies; 143 Verity Welstead/Narratives; 144l 'Windswept' Crispin & Gemma; 144-145 Interior Archive; 146 Paul Ryan/International Interiors (Architects: Moneo & Brock); 147 Jan Baldwin/Narratives; 148a Tim Street-Porter (NY Photographer); 148b IPC Syndication/Homes & Gardens; 149 Camera Press; 150l Deidi von Schaewen; 150ar Robert Harding Syndication/Inspirations/Lucinda Symons; 150cr IPC Syndication/ Homes & Gardens/Simon Upton; 150 br Robert Harding Syndication/ Inspirations/Gloria Nicol; 151r Robert Harding Syndication/ Inspirations; 152 Steve Sparrow/Houses & Interiors; 153 Tim Street-Porter; 154 Paul Ryan/International Interiors (Frances Halliday); 155 IPC Syndication/Homes & Gardens/Jan Baldwin; 156-157 Tim Street-Porter (Brindell Roberts); 158-160 Camera Press; 161 Cassina, Design: Philippe Starck; 162 Morgan River Ltd.; 164a Margolis; 164b Marianne Majerus; 165l Sharps Home Office; 165r Margolis; 166 Robert Harding Syndication/Inspirations; 167al Simon Butcher/Houses & Interiors; 167b Lars Hallen; 168 Sharps Home Office; 169 Richard Davies; 170-171 Zefa/Stockmarket; 172 IPC Syndication/Homes & Gardens; 173 Tome Leighton/John Lewis Department Stores; 176 Dennis Gilbert/Arcaid (Architects: Allford Hall Monaghan Morris).

Every effort has been made to trace the copyright holders and we apologize in advance for any unintentional omission and would be pleased to insert the appropriate acknowledgement in any subsequent editions.

Illustrations on page 97 and 163 by Phil Devine.

Publisher's acknowledgments We would like to thank the following: Paul Beauchamp (Zanotto), Keith Bambury, Alison Bolus, Jim Edwards (Morgan River), Sue Martin and Maggie McCormick.

Author's acknowledgments I owe a great many thanks to: Ellen Dupont, for both conceiving and encouraging this book; Joyce Mason, whose design brought it magically to life; Jane Chapman for being my safety net, reference source and sounding board as well as my editor; and Harry Aldwinckle, Jim Edwards and Maggie Heaney for their generous and invaluable help with research. For general and consistent professional support, I am also grateful to Angela Flitton and Lloyd Reynolds, and to my trusted agent and ally, Barbara Levy.